TERRA-COTTA FIGURINES AND MODEL VEHICLES

Bibliotheca Mesopotamica

Primary sources and interpretive analyses for the study of Mesopotamian civilization and its influences from late prehistory to the end of the cuneiform tradition

Editor: Giorgio Buccellati

Assistant Editors: John L. Hayes, Patricia Oliansky

Published Under the Auspices of
IIMAS
The International Institute for Mesopotamian Area Studies

BIBLIOTHECA MESOPOTAMICA
Volume 22

THE ORIENTAL INSTITUTE EXCAVATIONS AT SELENKAHIYE, SYRIA

Maurits van Loon, Editor

TERRA-COTTA FIGURINES AND MODEL VEHICLES

Harold Liebowitz

UNDENA PUBLICATIONS

Malibu 1988

TERRA-COTTA FIGURINES AND MODEL VEHICLES
by Harold Liebowitz

Eight hundred and twenty-five figurines and model vehicles were discovered during the 1965 and 1967 seasons of excavation at Tell Selenkahiye and Wreyde, Syria. The assemblage included human figurines, animal figurines, animal figurines with riders, and model wagons and chariots. This fascicle includes the following sections: (1) technique, (2) classification, (3) stratigraphy and style, (4) the regional character of the human figurines, (5) the function of the figurines, and (6) a catalogue divided into four subsections—(a) human figurines, (b) animal figurines, (c) animal and rider figurines, and (d) wagons and chariots.

Published with the assistance of AICF—The Ambassador International Cultural Foundation.

Library of Congress Card Catalog Number: 81-71738

ISBN 0-89003-104-5 (paper)
0-89003-105-3 (cloth)

(c) 1988 Undena Publications

All rights reserved. No part of this publication may be reproduced or transmitted in any form or by any means, electronic or mechanical, including photocopy, recording, or any information storage and retrieval system, without permission in writing from the publisher.

Undena Publications, P.O. Box 97, Malibu, California 90265 U.S.A.

FOREWORD

This fascicle is the first to appear in a series that will form the final report on the excavations carried out in 1965 and 1967 at Selenkahiye, in the Syrian Euphrates dam reservoir, by the University of Chicago Oriental Institute, thanks to permits granted by the Syrian General Direction of Antiquities and Museums and financial support provided by the National Science Foundation (GS-873 and GS-1416).

In the fall of 1965, while the Oriental Institute's Euphrates Valley Expedition was working at Mureybit on the east bank, Rudolph H. Dornemann carried out a preliminary sounding at Selenkahiye on the west bank. Ghislaine de Vallois van Loon was the expedition's photographer for that season. In the spring of 1967 the Euphrates Valley Expedition dug for three months at Tell Selenkahiye and its southern extension, Wreyde. Rudolph H. Dornemann, Alfred J. Hoerth, Stanislao Loffreda, and myself acted as site supervisors, Maude de Schauensee as registrar (also drawing many of the finds) and Isabelle de Vallois as photographer. Dr. Willem van Zeist and Dr. Pierre Ducos studied the plant and animal remains on the spot. We were greatly assisted by Mr. 'Abdurrazzaq Zaqzuq, who represented the General Direction of Antiquities and also supervised part of the excavation. I directed the expedition during both seasons.

The manuscript for this monograph, *Terra-Cotta Figurines and Model Vehicles*, by Harold Liebowitz, was submitted to me in 1975 for inclusion as a chapter in the report on results of our excavations at Tell Selenkahiye. While several important preliminary reports of excavations in Syria and studies of the art of Syria have been published since Dr. Liebowitz submitted his manuscript, the four-fold scheme for division of Middle Bronze Age (including what is now called Early Bronze IV) terra-cotta figurines into four regional manifestations—Palestine, coastal Syria, Orontes Valley, and Euphrates Valley—which he proposed in his dissertation (Ann Arbor, 1972) and before the General Meeting of the Archaeological Institute of America, in December, 1973, remains valid. While the inclusion of the new data would have enriched the following study, it would not have altered the results substantially.

The preliminary report on the excavation results, including appendices by Pierre Ducos and Willem van Zeist, appeared in *Annales Archéologiques Arabes Syriennes* 18 (1968), pp. 21-36. Shorter articles have appeared in the *Oriental Institute Reports* for 1965/66, pp. 20-22, 1966/67, pp. 13-15, and 1967/68, pp. 8-10 and 25; in *Archaeology* 22 (1969), pp. 276-277.

From 1971 to 1975 the excavation was continued by the University of Amsterdam's Euphrates Valley Expedition, again under my direction. The last preliminary report on its work has appeared in *Annals of the American Schools of Oriental Research* 44 (1979), pp. 97-112.

The remainder of the final report on the University of Chicago work at Selenkahiye will now be integrated into the report on its continuation by the University of Amsterdam, to appear in the near future as follows:

Architecture and Stratigraphy, by Maurits N. van Loon (1967) and Diederik J. W. Meijer (1972-75)

Graves and Finds from the Graves, by Maurits N. van Loon (1967) and Diederik J. W. Meijer (1972-75)

Pottery from the Houses Excavated in 1967, by Maurits N. van Loon

together with other chapters dealing with the 1972-75 results.

My thanks are due to Giorgio Buccellati and Marilyn Kelly-Buccellati for rendering publication in this modular format.

Maurits van Loon

Amsterdam, January, 1988

CONTENTS

FOREWORD by Maurits van Loon v
ABBREVIATIONS xiv

1. TECHNIQUE 1

2. CLASSIFICATION 4

    2.1. The Human Figurines 4
        2.1.1. Figurines with Hands Placed on the Chest: Types I-IV . . . 5
        2.1.2. Figurines with Extended Arm-Stumps 10
        2.1.3. Heads with Unidentifiable Body Types 12
        2.1.4. Unidentifiable Torsos and Heads 15
    2.2. The Animal Figurines 15
    2.3. Animal and Rider Figurines 18
    2.4. Model Wagons and Chariots 19

3. STRATIGRAPHY AND STYLE 22

4. THE REGIONAL CHARACTER OF THE HUMAN FIGURINES . . . 23

5. FUNCTION OF THE FIGURINES 27

    Catalogue A: Terra-Cotta Human Figurines 33
    Catalogue B: Terra-Cotta Animal Figurines 48
    Catalogue C: Animal and Rider Figurines 55
    Catalogue D: Chariots and Wagons 57

PLATES . . . . following page 60

ILLUSTRATIONS

FIGURINES WITH HANDS PLACED ON THE CHEST: TYPES I-IV

PLATE 1
1. SLK 67-526, Type IA. Complete, with circular concave base. Buff pottery, burned (?), grey at top.
2. SLK 67-684, Type IA. Bitumen applied to hair coils and the choker necklace.

PLATE 2
1. SLK 67-476, Type IA. Pinched pony tail with no decoration. Marking around outer edges of applied eye pellets.
2. SLK 67-125, Type IA. Head, left shoulder.
3. SLK 67-1, Type IA. Bust of female figurine, with prominent rectangular bun behind.
4. SLK 67-42, Type IA. Female figurine with pony tail, choker necklace.

PLATE 3
1. SLK 67-588, Type IA. Frontlet applied to the crown-like fringe, frontlet also applied to rectangular bun in back, small pendant at base of neck.
2. SLK 67-1082, Type IA. Bun with incisions representing hair.
3. SLK 67-998, Type IA. Choker necklace incised; pony tail incised.

PLATE 3A
1. SLK 67-146, Type IA. Dotted crown-like headdress, long diagonal incisions on pony tail.
2. SLK 67-939, Type IA. Crown-like headdress and bun, with dot decoration. Dot decoration also on top of head and back of crown headdress.
3. SLK 67-944, Type IA. Crown with vertically incised lines, double necklace at neck, vertical incised lines. Pony tail incised with herringbone pattern.

PLATE 4
1. SLK 67-116, Type I. Remains of tassle between the two necklaces. Back has three incised lines between shoulders.
2. SLK 67-390, Type I. Forearms and large hands slant upward.
3. SLK 67-1272, Type I. Arms and hands carelessly applied to chest.
4. SLK 67-1125, Type I. Large pendant (?) at base of neck.
5. SLK 67-3, Type I. Forearms and hand slant downward.

PLATE 5
1. SLK 67-207, Type IA. Large circular frontlet in center of crown, short pony tail behind.
2. SLK 67-595, Type IA. Long drop-shaped hair coils with dashes starting below ears, 2 holes in each ear. Plain long rectangular bun in back.
3. SI 1B 129, Type I. Prominent space between hands, forearms abbreviated.
4. SI 1B 89, Type I. Prominent space between hands, forearms absent.

PLATE 5A
1. SLK 67-910, Type I. Applied pellet necklace, long pony tail with applied pellet and incised decorations; bitumen applied to necklace.

PLATE 6
1. SLK 67-676, Type IB. Bun at back with 4 rows of diagonal dashes.
2. SLK 67-525, Type IB. Flat crown with vertical dashes. Short hair coils, large, rectangular undecorated bun.
3. SLK 67-1000, Type IB. Undecorated bun at back.
4. SLK 67-564, Type IC. Applied dot and dash eyes. Pony tail.
5. SLK 67-638, Type IC. Incised mouth with archaic smile, short, wide incisions on side curls; crown and parts of top of head decorated with punctuate dots; applied pellet eyes diagonally slashed; bun behind.

PLATE 7
1. SLK 67-607, Type ID. Undecorated pony tail curled under.

2. SLK 67-392, Type ID. Perforated between neck and hair curls.
3. SLK 67-952, Type IE. Applied pellet eyes with diagonal slashes.
4. SLK 67-382, Type IE. Tall broken headdress, eyebrows of applied bands with incisions.

PLATE 7A

1. SI 3 92, Type IE. Tall columnar headdress with 3 horizontally applied bands; no tresses, back of head plain.

PLATE 7B

1. SLK 67-930, Type IF. Arc-shaped, incised and stippled decoration above necklace; prominent eyebrows.

PLATE 8

1. SLK 67-860, Type IF. Badly worn.
2. SLK 67-1181, Type IF. Edges of headdress broken; slight tilt to the head; pony tail.
3. SLK 67-438, Type IH. Pincurls at each side of the face; pendant (?) above upper strand of the necklace; arms in low relief.

PLATE 9

1. SLK 67-945, Type IG. Necklace at base of neck and applied bands across shoulders; bitumen applied to back of head, arms curl up slightly.
2. SLK 67-1174, Type IJ. Crown headdress with applied and punctured pellets replacing tresses; choker necklace with diagonal incisions and 2 tassels (?); remains of bitumen on headdress, hair curls, and around eyes.
3. SLK 67-180, Type I. Broken crown headdress; punctuated eyes; ear flaps with 3 vertically aligned perforations; large pendant descends from below mouth; remains of short pony tail.

PLATE 10

1. SLK 67-425, Type II. Traces of bitumen at base of neck.
2. SLK 67-19, Type II. Arms which curve upward carelessly applied.
3. SLK 67-79, Type II. No trace of tresses at sides of neck.
4. SLK 67-477, Type II. Hands with 2 incisions on wrists curve upward between the applied pellet breasts.
5. SLK 67-666, Type II. Elaborate single strand necklace with attached pendants (?) above and below; grooves on chest upon which applied arms and hands curve upward.

PLATE 11

1. SLK 67-635, Type II. Bitumen applied to top of shoulder in antiquity to repair break; arms crudely applied to chest.
2. SLK 67-155, Type II. One applied pellet breast preserved.
3. SLK 67-1245, Type II. Small arm curves up around preserved pellet breast.
4. SLK 67-11, Type II. Arms curve upward between applied and punctured pellet breasts.
5. SI 1B 43, Type II. Upward curving hands exceptionally large.

FIGURINES WITH EXTENDED ARM-STUMPS

PLATE 12

1. SLK 67-695, Type IV. Conical headdress broken at top; oval-shaped applied eyes; applied eyebrows; horizontal ridge at back of head; bitumen applied to break at waist.
2. SLK 67-1128, Type IV. Oval-shaped applied eyes, applied eyebrows.
3. SLK 67-391, Type III. Bearded figure with hairy chest.
4. WRD 67-1, Type V. Neck to waist.
5. SLK 67-531, Type V. Bitumen applied to broken surfaces, to back of head, to forehead and necklace area.
6. SLK 67-623, Type V. Incised eyebrows.
7. SLK 67-2, untyped. Figurine with male, conical headdress, and with arms positioned as female figurines.

PLATE 13

1. SLK 67-704, Type V. Stubby projecting arms vertically perforated; oval, slightly concave base.
2. SLK 67-1123, Type V. Vertically pierced stubby arms project from elbow; joins head SLK 67-1085.
3. SLK 67-633, Type V. Arm Stumps vertically pierced.
4. SLK 67-993, Type V. One applied breast, 1 long necklace above breast near "armpit"; arm lost, but probably projected forward; back has pony tail from which incised lines radiate.
5. SI 1B 63, Type V. Arm stumps vertically pierced; vertical incisions on torso.
6. SI 1B 93, Type V. Tapering torso with insubstantial arm stumps.

PLATE 14

1. SI 1B 109, Type V. Upper body.
2. SLK 67-960, Type V. Vertical perforations in arm stumps.
3. SLK 67-978, Type V. Hole in top of extended arm stumps.
4. SI 1B 12, Type V. Perforated arm stump, vertical incisions on chest.
5. SLK 67-1253, Type V. Arm stumps not perforated, extended forward.
6. SLK 67-904, Type V. Short arms extended from elbow; rounded shoulders.

PLATE 15

1. WRD 67-2, Type V. Torso incised with contiguous triangles and vertical incisions topped by a horizontal incision.
2. SLK 67-938, Type V. Torso incised with contiguous triangles and vertical incisions topped by a horizontal incision.
3. SLK 67-144, Type V. Four horizontally aligned triangles.
4. SLK 67-294, Type V. Torso incised with contiguous right triangles.
5. SLK 67 700, Type V. Incised axe (?)
6. SLK 67-1011, Type V. Applied pellets representing necklace with dangling pendants or beads.
7. SLK 67-1092, Type V. Arm stumps vertically pierced; chest incised with vertical parallel lines.

PLATE 16

1. SLK 67-639, Type V. Tall conical headdress; incised eyebrows, single perforation in each ear lobe.
2. SLK 67-213, Type V. Conical headdress, perforated ears.
3. SLK 67-300, Type V. Conical headdress, perforated ears.
4. SI 1B 21, Type V. Conical headdress, perforated ears.
5. SLK 67-262, Type V. Conical headdress; perforated ears.
6. SI 1B 14, Type V. Head.
7. SLK 67-986, Type V. Ears not perforated; long neck.
8. SLK 67-859, Type V. Incised eyebrows; ears not perforated.
9. SLK 67-1085, Type V. Ears not perforated.
10. SLK 67-857, Type V. Conical headdress; ears perforated.

HEADS WITH UNIDENTIFIABLE BODY TYPES

PLATE 17

1. SLK 67-214, Type VI. Partial perforation through surviving arm stump.
2. SLK 67-1032, Type VI. Single perforation in each arm stump.
3. WRD 67-31, Type VI. Well preserved arm stump not perforated.
4. SLK 67-681, Type VI. Hair on nape of neck indicated by incised lines.

PLATE 18

1. S. Surf. 163, Type VII. Prongs of 4-pronged headdress broken away.
2. SI 1B 9, Type VII. Pellet folded over right ear.
3. SI 1B 61, Type VII. Applied pellet eyes with single diagonal slash in each.
4. SLK 67-620, Type VII. Tall, hollow headdress with 4 prongs, left ear broken, pellet folded over right ear.
5. SLK 67-399, Type VIII. Headdress hollow in center; "moustache" or -shaped pendant.
6. SLK 67-479, Type VIII. Badly worn; vertical dashes on collar-type necklace.

PLATE 19

1. SLK 67-1005, Type VII. Five-pronged headdress; horizontally aligned ears, prominent eyebrows of applied, curved strips.
2. SLK 67-422, Type VII. Four-pronged headdress; eyebrows of applied, curved strips of clay; left ear has pellet folded over top and bottom.
3. SLK 67-4, Type VII. Five-pronged headdress.
4. SLK 67-478, Type VII. Tall headdress, no secure evidence for prongs; prominent earflaps with central puncture in each.

PLATE 20

1. SLK 67-1132, Type IX. Beard and hair at nape of neck rendered by incisions.
2. SLK 67-1530, Type IX. Single pellet applied to left side of neck.

PLATE 21

1. SI 2 68, Type X. Beard and hair at nape of neck rendered by irregular, vertical incisions.

2. SI 2 76, Type X. Applied pony tail.
3. SLK 67-1291, Type XII. Bitumen at break of legs; long hair coils, right one curled under at top.
4. SLK 67-897, Type XI. Hips and stubby legs of kilted figurine.
5. SLK 67-604, Type XIIIA. Broad splaying base.
6. SLK 67-1084, Type XIIIA. Broad splaying base.
7. SLK 67-493, Type XIIIA. Narrow base.
8. SLK 67-880, Type XIIIA. Narrow base.

PLATE 22

1. SLK 67-378, Type XII. Torso hollow.
2. SLK 67-489, Type V. Complete except for head and left shoulder.

THE ANIMAL FIGURINES / ANIMAL AND RIDER FIGURINES

PLATE 23

1. SI 2 77, horse? Prominent erect mane.
2. SI 2 75, horse? Prominent erect mane with diagonal incisions.
3. SLK 67-958, horse?
4. SLK 67-1166, equid? Rectangular muzzle.

PLATE 24

1. SLK 67-936, horse. Long neck, erect mane, intact bridle.
2. SLK 67-295, horse. Hole in muzzle for bridle.
3. WRD 67-45, horse. Long neck with erect mane.
4. SLK 67-642, horse? Earflaps or blinkers cover part of each eye.
5. SLK 67-1109, horse? Slight ridge between broken ears may represent mane.

PLATE 25

1. SI 1B 24, bull. Face; muzzle broken away.
2. SI 1B 52, bull. Face; muzzle broken away.
3. SI 2 102, bull. Face; muzzle and most of horns broken away.
4. SLK 67-503, bull. Face broken away.
5. SLK 67-152, bull. No features on face.
6. SLK 67-227, bull. Muzzle broken away; applied, punctured pellet eyes.
7. SLK 67-216, bull. Thin, tapering muzzle, eyes applied, punctured pellets.

PLATE 26

1. SLK 67-427, bull? Thick, blunt muzzle.
2. SLK 67-374, bull? Blunt muzzle.
3. WRD 67-44, bull? Short body.
4. SLK 67-352, goat? Swept-back horns; incised chevron design on neck; dots for nostrils and eyes.

PLATE 27

1. SLK 67-542, donkey? Vertical incisions on front and side of neck.
2. SLK 67-256, sheep. Incised decorations on sides and front representing animal's coat.
3. SLK 67-502, ram? Prominent horns broken away, eyes and nostrils rendered by punctures.

PLATE 28

1. SLK 67-68, bird. Outspread wings, tall pedestal base.
2. SLK 67-699, bird. Highly stylized.
3. SLK 67-976, bird. Pedestal only.
4. SLK 67-592, animal and rider. Erect mane on head of animal.
5. SLK 67-683, animal and rider. Body of rider contiguous with neck of animal.
6. SLK 67-685, animal and rider. Headless animal with parts of rider's legs.
7. SLK 67-955, animal and rider. Tail complete, base of erect mane.

PLATE 29

1. SLK 67-668, bird. Bird on pedestal base, head missing.
2. SLK 67-15, bird. Only pedestal present.
3. SLK 67-460, bird. Head missing, incised wings and plumage.

PLATE 30

1. SLK 67-698, bird. Highly stylized, headless.
2. SLK 67-895, animal and rider. Left arm long and extended, right short and stumpy.
3. SLK 67-206, animal and rider. Only traces of rider remain.

PLATE 30A

1. SLK 67-1164, animal and rider. Upper part of rider figurine, extended left arm stump.

MODEL WAGONS AND CHARIOTS

PLATE 31

1. SLK 67-980, wagon. Back covered, front broken.
2. SLK 67-1248, chariot.
3. SLK 67-669, wagon.
4. SLK 67-953, chariot?

PLATE 32

1. SLK 67-894, wagon. Tubular axles, ring for attachment at front end, incised decorations on sides.
2. SLK 67-567, wagon.
3. SLK 67-873, wagon. Wagon fragment.
4. SLK 67-145, chariot/wagon. Chariot/wagon fragment.

PLATE 33

1. SLK 67-35, chariot/wagon. Front end with 2 apertures.
2. SLK 67-354, chariot. "Fish-tailed" front end.
3. SLK 67-33, wagon. Front bottom fragment, with axle housing.

PLATE 34

1. WRD 67-3, wagon. Incised with dotted triangles and herringbone pattern.

ABBREVIATIONS

AAS	*Annales Archéologiques de Syrie* (name later changed to *Annales Archéologiques Arabes Syriennes*)
Dunand, *Byblos I, II*	Maurice Dunand, *Fouilles de Byblos I, II,* Paris, 1937, 1954
Ingholt, *Rapport I, II*	Harald Ingholt, *Rapport preliminaire sur une campagne de fouilles à Hama (1931)*, Copenhagen, 1934; *Rapport preliminaire sur sept campagnes de fouilles à Hama (1932-38)*, Copenhagen, 1940
JNES	*Journal of Near Eastern Studies*
MAM	*Mission Archeologique de Mari*
MB	Middle Bronze Age
MDOG	*Mitteilungen der Deutschen Orient-Gesellschaft*
OIP	*Oriental Institute Publications*
S Surf	Selenkahiye 1965 Surface
SI	Selenkahiye 1965 Sounding I
SLK 67	Selenkahiye 1967 Excavation season
WRD 67	Wreyde (southern extension of Selenkahiye) 1967 excavation season

CHAPTER 1

TECHNIQUE

All of the human figurines from Selenkahiye and Wreyde are handmade, yet some of the large figurines have hollow, wheel-turned bases, and several figurines show evidence for the use of scraping tools.[1] None of the figurines are mold-made. While the figurines are generally solid, the torso fragments of two outsized figurines (SLK 67-378 [Pl. 22:1] and 1023) are hollow.

Anatomical and decorative details are usually rendered by means of pinching, application of pellets and strips, and incision. The noses are pinched and the eyes normally consist of applied pellets treated in a variety of ways. While in most instances the pellets are either punctured in the center or impressed with an inner circle and punctured in the center, the eyes of SLK 67-564, 638, 952; SI IB 10 and 61 consist of applied pellets with either a horizontal or diagonal slash in each pellet, and the eyes of SLK 67-180, 314, 1132 and 1530 lack applied pellets altogether, and consist of punctures in the clay.

Tresses are rendered by applied strips of clay, pin curls by applied pellets, and the thick ponytails by pinching and modelling. The infrequently featured breasts are represented by applied, punctured or unpunctured pellets. Most of the figurines wear necklaces, which predominantly consist of applied strips of clay representing single or multiple hanging strands, or choker necklaces. The necklaces are frequently decorated with short, randomly patterned incisions. Occasionally, the incisions are somewhat longer, and form parallel vertical or diagonal strokes. The necklace of one female figurine (SLK 67-910 [Pl. 5A])[1a] and the lower part of the necklace of a male figurine (SLK 67-1011 [Pl. 15:6]) consist of an arc of applied and punctured pellets. The lower part of the necklace of SLK 67-1092 consists of an arc of vertical incisions, and the choker necklace of SLK 67-298 consists of numerous punctures in the clay. The necklace of yet another figurine, SLK 67-531 (Pl. 12:5), consists of a curved band of bitumen, which was apparently applied after the necklace of applied strips broke away, leaving only tips of the necklace on the shoulders. In addition to the use of incision for the necklaces, incision is also used as a means of rendering the beard (SI 2 68; SLK 67-144, 294, 938, 1092, and WRD 67-2).

Bitumen occasionally appears to have been used decoratively as a coloring agent. On SLK 67-910 (Pl. 5A) the substance is applied to a necklace, while on SLK 67-1174 it is applied to pin curls. On SLK 67-1174 it is applied around the eyes and on SLK 67-945 it is applied to the back of the head. In other instances it appears to have been used to repair ancient breaks in the figurines. The latter usage is attested by the discovery of

---

[1] SLK 67-467, 901, 979, 1016. SLK 67-132 was also scraped with a tool and the downward direction of the strokes is evident.

[1a] Despite the nipples, this figurine may be male (cf. note 24) since the hands were apparently not placed on the chest (see, however, note 112a). The decoration on the back may represent a man's necklace counterweight, cf. note 29. —The Editor.

bitumen on broken surfaces, invisible when the figurines were complete.[2] In one instance, the missing head of a hollow figurine (SLK 67-378 [Pl. 22:1]) had been fitted into the torso and held in place with bitumen.

The color of the ware is most frequently buff. Eleven figurines are of orange-ware[3] and four of these orange-ware figurines are covered with a cream slip.[4] The ware of three figurines is greenish[5] and the ware of three other figurines is green.[6] The ware of one figurine (SLK 67-963) is gray and that of another (SLK 67-526) is also gray, and buff at the top.

The animal figurines are also hand-made. With the exception of SLK 67-1165, which is slightly hollow, all of the animal figurines are solid.

The eyes usually consist of either punctures in the clay (SI 2 75; SLK 67-289, 352, 502, 619, 1166) or applied and punctured pellets (SLK 67-206, 216, 277, 469, 1109, 1262). The eyes of two equid figurines (SI 2 77; SLK 67-936) are rendered by applied pellets with an inner impressed circle and central puncture, while the eyes of a long snouted bovid (SLK 67-427) are rendered by incised dotted circles. Nostrils are rendered by small punctures[7] and mouths by horizontal incisions.[8]

The animal figurines are usually undecorated. Yet, occasionally, incision and punctuate dots are used to render surface decoration. The neck of a donkey (?) SLK 67-542 is incised with vertical lines, possibly representing the mane, and the entire surface of a sheep (?) SLK 67-256 is incised with herringbone patterns. The surfaces of two animal figurines, SLK 67-568 and WRD 67-92, are decorated with punctures in the clay.

The color of the ware of the animal figurines is most frequently buff. However, three figurines (SLK 67-397, 1088, and 1243) are orange, and two of these orange figurines are covered with a cream slip (SLK 67-1088 and 1243). One figurine is greenish with a gray core (SLK 67-916), one is green (SLK 67-1545) and one is gray (SLK 67-1525).

The chariots are all hand made.[9] The bodies of the chariots and the wheels are made separately to enable the wheels to turn on their axles, which probably consisted of twigs. The chariot body is usually modelled from a single piece of clay. However, an additional piece of clay is applied to cover the back of SLK 67-980. As a rule, the axle housing at the base of the chariot is modelled from the same piece of clay used for the body of the chariot. Nevertheless, the axle housings of SLK 67-286 and 567 are attached from separate pieces of clay.

Half of the thirty-two chariot fragments are incised with geometric patterns. One of the incised examples (SLK 67-894) is also decorated with bitumen stripes which are carelessly applied.

---

[2] SLK 67-531, 543, 657, 1183. SLK 67-477 and 1170 are also suggestive of similar usage.

[3] SLK 67-79, 540b, 645, 666, 1016, 1246, 1322, 1517, 1541, 1553, 1556. SLK 67-8 is buff to orange.

[4] SLK 67-645, 1016, 1246, 1553. The ware of the latter two figurines is orange to light orange. It is noteworthy that the cream slip is applied exclusively to those figurines with orange or orange to light orange ware.

[5] SLK 67-127, 1017, 1530.

[6] SLK 67-680, 866, 957.

[7] SI 2 75, 77; SLK 67-289, 295, 352, 427, 502, 936, 1109, 1166, 1262.

[8] SI 2 75, 77; SLK 67-289, 295, 352, 427, 502, 649, 936, 1109, 1166, 1262.

[9] Several wheel-turned covered wagon fragments shaped like small pots, one side of which had been pushed in to form the floor, were found in 1974. Written communication, Maurits Van Loon, July, 1974.

1. Technique

The wheels are solid discs which taper toward the edges and with few exceptions have a hub on each side of the wheel. The hubs vary in size from small to prominent. As a rule, the hubs are modelled from the same piece of clay as the rest of the wheel, but the hub of SLK 67-832 appears to have been applied separately. All of the wheels are centrally pierced for the admittance of the axle. While the wheels are usually undecorated, incision is occasionally used to render details of their construction. SLK 67-981 has four incised lines representing spokes and SLK 67-863 shows faint traces of five of its eight spokes. The tread of SLK 67-1325 is indicated on one side by a faint incised circle at the outer edge.

The ware of the chariots and wheels is predominantly buff in color. However, the ware of one wheel (SLK 67-1523) is orange and the ware of two chariot fragments (SLK 67-836, 1488) is orange and is covered with a cream slip. Three chariot wheels (SLK 67-61, 497 and 498) are of gray ware.

CHAPTER 2

CLASSIFICATION

2.1. The Human Figurines

While differences among the figurines permit classification, the assemblage is recognizable as a distinct entity. With the exception of SLK 67-897, all of the figurines are pillar-shaped standing figures with splaying, slightly concave, circular or oval bases. The faces are characterized by prominent noses and the usual absence of either a mouth or chin.[10] The body is flat and usually plain, possibly intending to convey the impression of a fully clothed figure.[11] Details of dress are limited to the necklaces with which the figurines are frequently adorned. The usual plainness of the figurines is modified in several instances by incised decorations consisting of either abstract geometric patterns across the upper part of the torso or more naturalistic features such as a hairy chest and what in one instance may represent a crude rendering of a belt and dagger.[12]

The classification of the figurines is based on differing conventions for the rendering of the upper limbs and the heads. While variations also occur in the style of the necklaces, in the shape of the shoulders and in the presence or absence of incised decoration, paint or bitumen, only the rendering of the upper limbs and the head are significant for broad classification purposes. The other criteria occur without specific pattern or regularity.

The resultant types are grouped in accord with the treatment of the arms and hands rather than on the basis of the sex of the figurines, since the sex of the figurines is frequently uncertain due to the usual absence of genitalia or beards. The sex of the figurines is determined secondarily on the basis of the manner of treatment of the upper limbs and the coiffure or headdress, coincidentally the same criteria used to establish the basic typology of the figurine assemblage. As a rule, the figurines whose hands are placed on their chests and who wear elaborate coiffures[13] are identified as female, while those whose arm-stumps are extended in front of them are identified as male; yet some of the headless figurines of the latter type may be female. Those who wear

---

[10] A mouth is indicated in only two instances (SLK 67-382 and 391) and a chin is indicated in only three instances (SI 2 79; SLK 67-398 and 945).

[11] Cf. Maurits Van Loon, "First Results of the 1967 Excavations at Tell Selenkahiye," *Annales Archeologiques Arabes Syriennes,* XVIII (1968) p. 28. Yet the plain treatment may represent a reduction of detail and not necessarily figures in long robes.

[12] See Types III and V, below.

[13] The heads of the Type II figurines are missing in every instance. Yet, it is likely that they also had elaborate coiffures.

conical headdresses are identified as male.[14]

2.1.1. Figurines with Hands Placed on the Chest: Types I - IV

Type I: (67 examples:[15] S Surf 160; SI IB (31), 60, 89, 129; SI 2 79; SI 3-92; SLK 67-1, 3, 42, 116, (125), 127, 146, 163, (207), 218, 382, 390, 392, 401, 438, 476, 484, 487 (525), 526, (532), 553, 561, (564), 566, (588), (595), 596, 606, 632, 638, (645), (676), 680, 684, 690, 856, 860, 862, 910, 930, 945, 952, (998), 1000, 1009, 1027, 1040, 1041, 1121, 1125, 1167, 1168, 1181, 1224, 1234, 1272, 1322, 1324; WRD 67-43 [Pls. 1-9])

The upper part of the torso of the Type I figurine is usually triangular.[16] The upper arm of the figurine follows the contour of the torso, and the forearms which lay across the chest are attenuated. Frequently, the forearms are completely absent. The hands, with fingers rendered by incisions, are positioned either horizontally, or slant upward or downward in accord with the slant of the forearms when the latter are rendered. The wrists are often incised, perhaps to indicate bracelets. Only two Type I figurines (SLK 67-910, Pl. 5A; S Surf 160) have breasts, which consist of small applied and punctured pellets.

Type I is subdivided on the basis of variations in the treatment of the coiffure. The basic components of the coiffure are tresses (of varying sizes and treatments) composed of strips of clay applied to each side of the face, a crown-like fringe across the forehead, pin curls of varying degrees of prominence and either a thick ponytail or rectangular protuberance at the back of the head, probably representing hair folded over some sort of supporting comb.

Type IA: (18 examples: SI IB-70; SI 2 27; SLK 67-1, 42, 47, 51, 125, 146, 207, 476, 526, 588, 595, 605, 684, 690, 939, 998)[17]

The shoulder-length tresses are substantial and the crown-like fringe across the forehead immediately above the eyes, is prominent. The hair at the back of the head is rendered either as a thick pony tail (SI 2 27; SLK 67-42, 207, 476, 526 [Pl. 1:1], 595, 998), usually with short incisions to indicate the hair, or as a rectangular protuberance (SLK 67-1 [Pl. 1:2], and SI IB 51).

---

[14] Cf. below, pp. 28-30.

[15] Type I is subdivided into subtypes 1A - 1J on the basis of variations in the manner of treatment of the coiffure. All Type I figurines, including those which can and cannot be subdivided, are included in this Type I list. Figurines sufficiently well-preserved to permit assignment of a subtype appear in their appropriate subtype listing. The arms of the figurines whose field numbers appear in parentheses are not preserved, yet the figurines are attributed to this type on the basis of other stylistic considerations, i.e., the nature of the necklaces and other minor details.

[16] Only three examples are rectangular-shaped (S. Surf. 160; SLK 67-484 and 1125).

[17] The attribution of SI 1B 70 and SI 2 27 to this type is based on the small part of the hair curl preserved at the neck.

The eyes of Type IA are usually rendered by applied pellets with an inner impressed circle and central puncture, though the eyes of SLK 67-125 and 476 (Pl. 2:1, 2) are rendered by applied and punctured pellets without an inner impressed circle.

Several Type IA figurines have distinct characteristics which set them apart from the other Type IA figurines. The outer edges of the crown-like fringe of SLK 67-125, 476, and 526 (Pl. 1:1) curve upward, recalling horns on the Mesopotamian divine images. A pellet with an inner impressed circle and central puncture is applied to the crown-like fringe of SLK 67-207 (Pl. 5:1), 588 (Pl. 3:1) and 595 (Pl. 5:2) and represents a type of frontlet.[18] A similar pellet is applied to the back of the head of SLK 67-588 (Pl. 3:1).

SLK 67-146, 595, 963, and 1082 vary from the norm, yet are attributed to Type IA. SLK 67-595 (Pl. 5:2) differs since the upper part of its tresses are replaced with ear-flaps with two vertically aligned perforations in each, probably for the attachment of earrings. SLK 67-998 (Pl. 3:3) varies in the extremely prominent crown-like fringe which is decorated with two rows of closely placed fine vertical incisions. SLK 67-1082 (Pl. 3:2) is distinguished by the thin strip of clay (perhaps representing poorly rendered eyebrows) applied to the space usually absent between the eyes and the crown-like fringe, and by the prominent pin curls at the side of the face. SLK 67-146 (Pl. 3:4) and 939 (Pl. 3:5)[19] vary because of the absence of the tresses at the sides of the face. SLK 67-963 departs most radically from the norm for the type. The tresses of SLK 67-963 are insubstantial in contrast with the prominent ringlets. The unusual quality of the figurine is emphasized by the absence of a crown-like fringe and by the way in which the gently undulating tresses cascade from beneath the figurine's large eyes of applied and punctured pellets.

SI IB 10; SLK 67-941 and 994 (Pl. 3:6) may be viewed as degenerate examples of the type. While SI IB 10 has ringlets and insubstantial tresses, it lacks both the fringe on the forehead and either the thick ponytail or rectangular protuberance at the back of the head and its eyes are rendered by applied pellets which are carelessly horizontally slashed. SLK 67-941 also lacks the fringe of the forehead and its ponytail is carelessly rendered. The tresses of SLK 67-994 are carelessly incised, yet the figurine is of interest since the thick ponytail at the back of its head is parted. SLK 67-47 with a flat crown-like fringe, insubstantial tresses, short locks behind the tresses and a bun at the back of the head is another crude example of Type IA.

---

[18] A frontlet held in place by a double fillet is found on the forehead of a naked hero grasping the tails of two lions on the base of a cup from the Protoliterate period found at Tell Agrab (Henri Frankfort, *The Art and Architecture of the Ancient Orient* [Baltimore, 1963] pl. 6). The frontlet of the naked hero on another cup from the same period is less well preserved, but unmistakable (*ibid.*, pl. 6 C). The naked hero, though not necessarily a god, is no mere mortal (*ibid.*, p. 12). Thus, the frontlet is related to the supernatural realm. Several oval or round silver frontlets tied over the foreheads of the dead were found in graves at Selenkahiye.

[19] SLK 67-939 closely parallels a figurine from Habuba Kabira (cf. below, n. 55). For a full discussion of parallels to the Selenkahiye figurines, see the section on regionalism, below.

2. Classification

Type IB: (4 examples: SLK 67-525, 645, 676, 1000)

The style of the coiffure of the type (Pl. 6:1-3) is similar to that of Type IA except that the tresses are shorter and the hair at the back of the head is, with one possible exception,[20] consistently rendered as a rectangular protuberance.

Type IC: (4 examples: SI 2 79; SLK 67-564, 638, 856)

The tresses of SI 2 79, SLK 67-564 (Pl. 6:4), SLK 67-638 (Pl. 6:5), and SLK 67-856 are insubstantial and adhere to the sides of the face and neck, thus slanting in rather than falling straight. SLK 67-564 (Pl. 6:4) and 638 (Pl. 6:5) are distinguished by their eyes of applied and slashed pellets. SI 2 79 is exceptional since it has a pronounced chin.

Type ID: (2 examples: SLK 67-392, 607)

The figurines of this type (Pl. 7:1, 2) are related to those of Type IA yet differ in their overall appearance because of the parallel diagonal incisions on the tresses, which give them more of the appearance of curls than free-flowing strands of hair, and because of the contiguous choker necklaces. Moreover, the eyes of both of these figurines, which consist of applied and punctured pellets without inner impressed circles, are more prominent than the eyes of the figurines of Type IA and in their staring quality they recall the Early Dynastic stone statuettes from Tell Asmar.[21]

Type IE: (3 examples: SI 3 92; SLK 67-382, 952)

This type is characterized by tall headdresses. SI 3 92 (Pl. 7A:1) is particularly distinguished by a tall columnar headdress encircled by three horizontally applied bands of clay. While SI 3 92 lacks tresses, the tresses of the two extremely crude figurines, SLK 67-382 (Pl. 7:4) and 952 (Pl. 7:3) are insubstantial and carelessly incised. The pin curls of both of these figurines, rendered by contiguous applied pellets, are more prominent than the tresses. SLK 67-382 is distinguished by the incised mouth and by the eyebrows of applied strips of clay which meet at the bridge of the nose in typical Mesopotamian fashion. The backs of the heads of the three figurines of the type are plain.

Type IF: (3 examples: SLK 67-860, 930, 1181)

This type, represented by only three heads, is characterized by the crown-like fringe on

---

[20] The gathered hair at the back of the head of SLK 67-645 is broken away and may have been rendered as a thick ponytail.

[21] Henri Frankfort, *Sculpture of the Third Millennium B.C. from Tell Asmar and Khafajah*, OIP XLIV (Chicago, 1939), Pls. 1, 4. The relatively prominent perforations in the applied pellets of the Selenkahiye examples correspond to the huge pupils of the eyes in the Tell Asmar stone statuettes.

the forehead and by the ponytail. The tresses and frequently accompanying pin curls found on the other subtypes are absent. The eyes of SLK 67-860 (Pl. 8:1), though worn, are applied pellets with inner impressed circles and central punctures, while the eyes of SLK 67-1181 (Pl. 8:2) are applied pellets with central punctures. SLK 67-930 (Pl. 7B) is unique because of the stippled and incised decoration on the figurines's neck above the necklace, and because of the prominent eyebrows consisting of thin, applied strips of clay, and applied pellet ears with a single puncture in each.[21a]

Type IG: (1 example: SLK 67-945)

The figurine of Type IG (Pl. 9:1) is distinguished by three contiguous pellets representing pin curls applied to the sides of the head, by the flattened crown-like fringe on the forehead and by the plain back of the head which lacks either ponytail or any hairdo. The eyes are rendered by applied and punctured pellets. The area framed by the upward slanting arms is filled with four rows of short vertical incisions separated by horizontal incisions which possibly represent an elaborate garment.

Type IH: (2 examples: SLK 67-438, 1027)

This type represented by only two examples (SLK 67-438 [Pl. 8:3] and SLK 67-1027) is characterized by frontally pierced contiguous pellets applied to the sides of the head.[22] These pellets may either represent the ears, from which earrings dangled, or the coiffure, with the hair set in short horizontal curls. Each of the figurines has a crown headdress and a thick ponytail. The eyes of each of the figurines are rendered as applied and punctured pellets.

Type IJ: (1 example: SLK 67-1174)

The outstanding feature of this figurine (Pl. 9:2) is the series of contiguous applied and punctured pellets surrounding the face.[23] Small pellets, representing horizontal curls, are placed on either side of the neck and head, and larger pellets, dwarfing the small applied and punctured pellet eyes, represent the crown-like fringe. The first, third, and fifth pellets of the crown-like fringe have a single perforation in each, and the second and

---

[21a] Despite the ponytail, this figurine may be male (cf. Type V) on account of the emphasized eyebrows and earlobes and the—broken—conical headgear and arm-stumps bent forward. —The Editor.

[22] SLK 67-438 has three pellets on its preserved left side and ALK 67-1027 has two pellets on each side. SLK 67-180 has prominent, pinched ear-flaps with three vertically aligned perforations in each. Though superficially similar to Type I because of the perforations, it differs radically and is excluded from the type. SLK 67-595 also has ear-flaps with vertically aligned perforation, which superficially identify the figurine with Type IH, yet this figurine is closer in style to Type IA.

[23] The discovery of a close parallel to this figurine at Habuba Kabira supports the assignment of a distinct type to this figurine. Cf. below, nn. 57-63.

fourth have two perforations in each. The importance of the crown is emphasized by the size of the five pellets constituting the crown and by the deliberate alternation in the number of perforations. Note also how the top of the head is pushed in to force the crown forward. The hair at the back of the head, which descends from below the indentation, is marked with vertical and diagonal incisions.

Type II: (11 examples: SI IB 43, 100; SLK 67-11, 19, 79, 155, 425, 477, 635, 666, 1245 [Pls. 10, 11])

The arms of the figurines of this type curve upward across the chest in contrast with the arms of the Type I figurines which follow the outer edge of the torso and angle in sharply. The hands of six of the figurines (SI IB 32 [Pl. 11:5]; SLK 67-11 [Pl. 11:4]; 19 [Pl. 10:2]; 79 [Pl. 10:3]; 425 [Pl. 10:1]; 666 [Pl. 10:5]) are vertically and contiguously aligned in a non-clasping gesture. Five of the eleven Type II figurines (SI IB 100, SLK 67-11 [Pl. 11:4]; 155 [Pl. 11:2]; 477 [Pl. 10:4]; 1245 [Pl. 11:3]) have breasts. The breasts of three of the figurines consist of small applied and punctured pellets (SI IB 100; SLK 67-11, 477), and the one surviving breast of SLK 67-144 (Pl. 11:2) and 1245 (Pl. 11:3) consists of a small applied, unpunctured pellet. On the basis of the relatively high percentage of Type II figurines with breasts, and on the basis of the upward curve of the arms, it is certain that a breast-supporting, rather than a hand-clasping position is intended.

The nature of the heads which belong to these figures cannot be determined since the heads are consistently missing.

Type III: (1 example: SLK 67-391 [Pl. 12:3])

This type is represented by the upper part of a single figurine (Pl. 12:3). The figurine's diminutive left arm, ending in a hand with fingers delineated by short incisions, is applied to its chest. Short vertical incisions seem to indicate hair on the figurine's shoulders and chest. The back is decorated with two concentric arcs of irregularly incised lines which represent either hair or some type of garment. The figurine has a low forehead, a pinched nose, eyes of applied pellets with a horizontal incision in the preserved right eye, ears of vertically pinched applied pellets, a grooved mouth and a beard and mustache indicated by short incised strokes. The figurine's hair is also indicated by incised strokes. The beard and mustache identify the figurine as a male.

Type IV: (2 examples: SLK 67-695, 1128)

This type is represented by the upper part of one figurine (SLK 67-695 [Pl. 12:1]) and by the head of another figurine (SLK 67-1128 [Pl. 12:2]). Both figurines wear conical caps. They have wide thin eyebrows, eyes of oval-shaped applied pellets with horizontal incisions, and prominent noses. The face is framed by the eyebrows and the lower jaw which is prominently rendered by pinching.

The slender upper arms of SLK 67-695 descend vertically following the contour of the torso. The hands angle in horizontally. The diminutive breasts of applied, unpunctured pellets are set far apart near the armpits of this otherwise obviously male figurine.[24]

2.1.2. Figurines with Extended Arm-Stumps

Type V: (38 examples: SI IB 12, 63, 93, 95, 109, 125; SI 2 80; SLK 67-18, 45, 144, 213, 294, 299, 489, 531, 550, 551, 560, 562, 583, 633, 700, 704, 904, 938, 957, 960, 978, 993, 995, 1011, 1031, 1092, 1117, 1123, 1253; WRD 67-1, 2; 14 heads attributable to this type were also found: SI IB 14, 21; SLK 67-148, 243, 262, 300, 485, 623, 639, 857, 859, 986, 1085 [Pls. 12-16])[25]

The figurines of Type V are characterized by arm-stumps which are extended in front of the body and by the conical headdress.[26] The arm-stumps project from the body either from the shoulder height or from below shoulder height. The shoulders of the figurines with arm-stumps projecting at shoulder height are usually slightly rounded (SLK 67-489 [Pl. 22:2]), while the shoulders of the figurines with arm-stumps projecting below shoulder height are usually square (SLK 67-704 [Pl. 13:1]). The ends of the arm-stumps, particularly those that project below shoulder height, are often vertically perforated and are likely to have held weapons such as maceheads or axes.[27]

Six of the Type V figurines have incised decorations. The incised decorations on four of the figurines (SLK 67-144, 294, 938; WRD 67-2 [Pl. 15:1])[28] are closely related to one another and are characterized by contiguous triangles below which are a series of vertical lines connected on top by a horizontal line. SLK 67-938 (Pl. 15:2) and WRD 67-2 (Pl. 15:1) have three contiguous triangles; SLK 67-294 (Pl. 15:4) has two large preserved, contiguous right triangles; and SLK 67-144 (Pl. 15:3) has four non-contiguous acute angles placed slightly above a horizontal line just above the break in the figurine. Two of the better preserved figurines (SLK 67-294 [Pl. 15:4], 938 [Pl. 15:2]) are decorated below the vertical incisions. SLK 67-294 is decorated with a partially preserved arc with two radial incisions and SLK 67-938 with the angular top of an indeterminate object. The lesser preserved figurines (SLK 67-144 [Pl. 15:3]; WRD 67-2 [Pl. 15:2]) probably had similar decorations but the lower section of each of these figurines is broken away.

A fifth figurine (SLK 67-1092 [Pl. 15:7]) is decorated with an arc-shaped series of parallel vertical incisions congruous with the shape of the necklace of applied bands. A similar

---

[24] The indication of diminutive breasts or nipples on this and other apparently male figurines (WRD 67-1; SLK 67-993) implies that the presence or absence of breasts cannot be used to determine the sex of the figurines.

[25] The arms of SLK 67-310, 957, 1008 are missing. Yet, these figurines may belong to Type V.

[26] Only one figurine of the type (SLK 67-531 [Pl. 12:5]) was found with the head still attached. Though the headdress is broken, it can reasonably be reconstructed as a conical headdress. Another figurine (SLK 67-857 [Pl. 16-10]) with upwardly slanting shoulders and with conical headdress is broken above the arms and provides less convincing evidence for the identification of figurines with extended arm-stumps, with the numberous heads with conical headdress. SLK 67-2 (Pl. 12:7) with its forearms and hands slanting upward across the chest, but with a typical Type V head, may be an exception.

[27] See below, pp.

[28] SLK 67-144 is broken just below the incised triangles, but the figurine was probably also incised with vertical lines connected on top by a horizontal line.

decoration is incised on the figurine's back from shoulder to shoulder. The preserved right side of a sixth figurine (SLK 67-700, [Pl. 15:5]) is incised with a diagonally oriented oval, bisected by an incised line which extends beyond the oval a short way to the break at the waist. The decoration may represent either a dagger, macehead, or possibly even an axe. The back of the figurine is decorated with four incisions which radiate from the back of the figurine's neck, and which may represent hair.[29]

The heads of the Type V figurines are essentially homogeneous. They are beardless and wear conical-shaped headdresses incised with short, vertical strokes. The eyes are rendered either by applied and punctured pellets or by pellets of an inner impressed circle and central puncture. Three of the heads (SLK 67-589, 623, 639)[30] have incised eyebrows which meet above the bridge of the nose in characteristic Mesopotamian fashion. The ears, which are a prominent feature of these figurines, are rendered as pierced earlobes with a single perforation in each (S1 1B 21; SLK 67-243, 262, 300, 639, 857 [Pl. 16:4, 2, 5, 3, 1, 10]). The ears of SI IB 14 ([Pl. 16:6]; SLK 67-623, 859 [Pl. 16:8], 986 [Pl. 16:7]) are not pierced. However, the flaps of SLK 67-623 and 859 representing the earlobes are simply folded over. The nose is prominent and the mouth is absent.[31]

A small, badly-worn figurine with a conical-shaped head, but with a pinched ponytail (SLK 67-533) may be a variant of Type V. Several figurines (SLK 67-550, 560, 957) with stubby arm-stumps extended to one side and the other widened arm-stump extended to the other side, may also belong to Type V, though they may be riders broken away from the backs of their equids.

Type VI: (4 examples: SLK 67-214, 681, 1032; WRD 67-31)

The figurines of this type which are closely related to the Type V figurines, are characterized by pointed arm-stumps, outstretched sideways. The bodies of SLK 67-214, 1032 and WRD 67-31 (Pl. 17:1-3) which are probably male,[32] are plain. The body of SLK 67-681 (Pl. 17:4) is elaborately decorated with: (1) diminutive breasts of applied and punctured pellets; (2) a type of harness composed of applied strips of clay going over the shoulders, joining in front and back and connecting up with a strap around the waist which is pulled upward in the center in the front and back; (3) a series of short incisions and punctures around the waist, forming a primitive rosette in back; (4) four short vertical incisions in front, below the incisions around the waist; (5) two diagonal incisions, perhaps representing the pubic triangle; and (6) several faint incisions on the back of the neck probably representing shoulder length hair.

---

[29] The incisions on the back may represent the counterweight which is a regular feature of necklaces in the second millennium. Written communication, Maurits Van Loon, July 20, 1974.

[30] SLK 67-300 appears to have eyebrows rendered by a raised band in low relief.

[31] SLK 67-623 and 857 vary slightly from the norm. The headdress of the former is not incised and the incised lines on the latter descend the figurine's back and probably represent hair.

[32] The arm-stumps of SLK 67-1032 are vertically pierced and the preserved right arm of SLK 67-214 is partially vertically pierced. The situation with WRD 67-31 is uncertain since its right arm is broken at the shoulder, and its left arm is broken at the end. These figurines are more closely related to those of Type V which have vertically pierced arm stumps and are identified as male figurines than to the series of obviously female MB II figurines with outstretched arm stumps from the Orontes Valley (for example cf. Leonard Woolley, *Alalakh: An Account of the Excavations at Tell Atchana in the Hatay, 1937-1949* (London, 1955), [Pl. LIV g.]).

2.1.3. Heads with Unidentifiable Body Types[33]

Type VII: (9 examples: S. Surf. 163; SI IB 9, 61; SLK 67-4, 442, 478, 620, 855, 1005)

This type is distinguished by the headdress, eyebrows and ears. The figurines wear tall, pronged crowns.[34] With the exception of SI IB 61 (Pl. 18:3) whose eyes are rendered by applied pellets with a single, slanting incision in each pellet, the eyes are rendered by applied pellets with an inner impressed circle and central puncture in each. The eyebrows are prominent and are rendered in four instances (SLK 67-442, 478 [Pl. 19:2, 4], 855, 1005 [Pl. 19:1]) by arc-shaped strips of clay[35] applied above the eyes and meeting above the bridge of the nose in typical Mesopotamian fashion. SLK 67-478 (Pl. 19:4) which has a tall cylindrical headdress decorated with a double circle of shallow incisions on the top of its preserved portion, and eyebrows of two contiguous applied strips of clay, may also belong to Type VII. Yet since the top of the headdress is broken away and no trace of a prong is preserved, the typological identification is tentative. The eyebrows of S. Surf. 163 (Pl. 18:1) are rendered by two applied strips with diagonal incisions in each, and meet at the bridge of the nose. The eyebrows of yet another figurine (SI IB 9 [Pl. 18:2]) are rendered by a series of diagonal incisions in the clay. The Type VII heads consistently feature ears, rendered either as long fleshy lobes (S. Surf. 163; SI IB 61; SLK 67-4 [Pl. 18:1, 3; 19:3]) as pinched flaps folded in front either horizontally (SI IB 9; SLK 67-620 [Pl. 18:2, 4]) or vertically on top and bottom (SLK 67-442 [Pl. 19:2]) or as prominent, horizontally pinched flaps (SLK 67-1005 [Pl. 19:1]).

Type VIII: (4 examples: SLK 67-399, 479, 598, 1515)

The figurines of this rather heterogeneous type are characterized by cylindrical headdresses, ear-flaps with single perforations in each and eyebrows which meet above the bridge of the nose in typical Mesopotamian fashion.

The cylindrical headdresses are treated in a variety of ways. The headdresses of SLK 67-399 (Pl. 18:5) and 479 (Pl. 18:6) are vertically striated, the headdress of SLK 67-1515 is decorated with short vertical incision, the hollow headdress of SLK 67-598 is decorated with random vertical incisions in front and horizontal incisions on the sides. (SLK 67-478 [Pl. 19:4], decorated with a double circle of shallow incisions near its top, may possibly belong to Type VIII, but has tentatively been identified with Type VII.) With the exception

---

[33] Only the heads of figurines of these types were discovered and it cannot be determined with certainty to which, if any, of the unknown body types these heads belong.

[34] A figurine of this type discovered at Selenkahiye in 1974 (SLK 74-H 162) had his right fist extended forward and pierced, and his left hand across his chest and holding a whip (?) folded over his shoulder. Written communication by Maurits Van Loon, July 20, 1974. Cf. the copper support featuring a nude male with a four-pronged crown from the Temple Oval at Khafaje (Frankfort, *op. cit.* [above, n. 21] [Pl. 98]).

[35] The eyebrows of SLK 67-1005 consist of contiguous, concentric strips of clay. The eyebrows of the remaining three figurines may have also been comprised of contiguous concentric strips of clay, but the additional strips may have disappeared.

of SLK 67-479 (Pl. 18:6),[35a] whose eyes are rendered by applied and punctured pellets, the eyes are rendered as applied pellets with an inner impressed circle and central puncture. SLK 67-399 (Pl. 18:5) has a prominent ʌ-shaped pendant on its long neck,[35b] while SLK 67-479 and 1515 wear choker necklaces.[36]

Type IX: (3 examples: SLK 67-314, 1132, 1530)

The type is characterized by eyes rendered by punctures in the clay, and headbands consisting of a single band of clay applied to the head above the ears and extending from ear to ear. While the applied crown of the well-preserved head (SLK 67-1530 [Pl. 20:2]) is unadorned, the crown of SLK 67-1132 (Pl. 20:1) is decorated with two incised grooves. Though badly worn, SLK 67-314 appears to belong to Type IX.

Type X: (2 examples: SI 2 68, 76)

The figurines of this type (Pl. 21:1, 2) are typified by rounded skulls, low foreheads and the absence of either a headdress or an elaborate coiffure.[37] The combination of these characteristics emphasizes the visual effect of the pinched noses and the applied pellet eyes with inner impressed circles and renders them unusually prominent.

2.1.4. Unidentifiable Torsos and Heads

Type XI: (2 examples: SLK 67-897, 971)

This type is best represented by a figurine fragment (SLK 67-897 [Pl. 21:4]) preserved from the hips to the feet. The figurine which appears to wear a kilt is unique, since its thick-set legs are differentiated by vertical grooves in front and back. SLK 67-971 is also assigned to this type since the rectangular torso fragment also has remains of what appears to be parts of legs.

Type XII: (30 examples: SI I 30, 36; SI IB 17, 25, 83; SLK 67-8, 86, 147, 151, 208, 251, 261, 279, 303, 378, 398, 483, 486, 505, 555, 636, 646, 665, 674, 854, 877, 885, 990, 997, 1291 [Pls. 21-22])

[35a] Despite the lack of tresses—probably due to breakage—and the unusually tall vertical incisions on the crown-like fringe, this head is likely to have belonged to Type IA. The tip of the fringe is partly intact and the back of the head clearly displays a ponytail. —The Editor.

[35b] The pendant may be meant to render an inverted crescent. The 1972-75 excavations at Selenkahiye yielded stone and clay inverted crescent pendants as well as male figurines with tall headgear and inverted crescent pendants, perhaps representing the moon god. —The Editor.

[36] The remaining two figurines are broken above the point where the necklace is usually found.

[37] The faintly incised lines on SI 2 68 represent the beard and hair, and a skimpy strip of clay applied to the back of the head of SI 2 76 represents a ponytail. Yet the bald quality of these heads is dominant.

This type includes figurines too crude, worn, or fragmentary to warrant secure classification. An extremely crude figurine, SLK 67-1291 (Pl. 21:3) with eyes of applied and punctured pellets, long hair curls, a body rectangular in section and without arms is ultimately related to Type 1A-F. The five heads, SI I 30, 36; SI IB 17, 25, and 83 are also ultimately related to Type 1A-F. The badly worn head, SLK 67-558 with short tresses and some incision on the back of the head may ultimately belong to Type 1B. SLK 67-8, the neck and lower part of a head, with only one-half of its eyes and its right ear preserved may be attributable to Type V.

SLK 67-877 with eyes of applied pellets with inner impressed circles and central punctures may have had a tall open crown, but the figurine is broken above the eyes. SLK 67-147 also has the remains of a pinched hollow crown. This figurine has eyes of applied and punctured pellets with an inner impressed circle, pierced earlobes, a perforation at the base of the neck and a perforation in the forehead. (Cf. SLK 67-207, 588, 895 which have "frontlets" applied to their crown-like fringes of their foreheads.)

SLK 67-398 is distinguished by its chin, the flattish plane of the oval face, the long thin nose and the diminutive eyes of applied and punctured pellets with central punctures. SLK 67-505 has an extremely long neck, a small, poorly preserved head and one preserved applied pellet eye. SLK 67-303 is badly worn and its nose is missing. It has large eyes of applied and punctured pellets and a flat head with a chevron decoration pointing in the direction of the figure's left ear. The head, SLK 67-151, has eyes of applied pellets.

SLK 67-5, 261, 854, and 855 are chest fragments retaining parts of the necklaces, but these fragments cannot be classified, though they are possibly attributable to either Type I or V. SLK 67-486 with its preserved right hand vertically positioned on the chest may belong to Type II. SLK 67-483, a chest fragment with a two-strand necklace and the remains of an applied arm along the contour of the chest, curving in, but lacking a hand with incised fingers, may be ultimately related to Type I-III.

The generally shapeless, headless figurines with stubby shoulders and no arms (SLK 67-279 and 281) must also be attributed to Type XII. While SLK 67-378 (Pl. 22:1), 646, 674, and 990 are preserved from the shoulders to the pedestal base, they cannot be securely identified since their arms are missing, though they may be candidates for Type V.

Type XIII

This type includes bases (Type XIIIA) and lower torso fragments (Type XIIIB).

Type XIIIA: (92 examples: SI I 31, 37, 47; SI IB 19, 45, 48, 49, 50, 64, 72, 73, 74, 84, 85, 96-98, 106, 108, 110, 132, 143; SI 2 65, 71, 78, 91; SLK 67-69, 10, 12, 13, 16, 17, 32, 62, 66, 67, 70, 84, 120, 130, 131, 132, 154, 167, 204, 236, 239, 241, 247, 249, 263, 312, 313, 577, 585, 323, 339, 353, 404, 408, 441, 463, 464, 466, 467, 490, 491, 492, 493, 494, 527, 534, 537, 540, 543, 547, 549, 572, 574, 576, 587, 591, 604, 605, 610, 621, 680, 1084; WRD 67-36, 294, 564 [Pl. 21])

This type includes bases and varying sized parts of the torsos. Most of the bases splay to a sufficient degree to permit the figurines to stand. SLK 67-130, 241, 604 (Pl. 21:5), 610, 591, 1084 (Pl. 21:6) and WRD 67-36 splay particularly prominently, while SLK 67-493 (Pl.

21:7), 605, and 880 (Pl. 21:8) splay slightly and do not permit the figurines to adequately balance themselves.

Type XIIIB: (26 examples: SI I 12-117; S. Surf. 158; SI IB 20, 55, 127, 136, 131, 142, 144; SI 2 111, 158; SLK 67-21, 128, 158, 240, 315, 348, 594, 597, 609, 623)

This type includes fragments of the lower parts of the torso corresponding to the waist, hips and legs.

2.2. The Animal Figurines

More than a hundred and seventy animal figurines were found at Selenkahiye and Wreyde during the 1967 season. Only a fraction of these are complete or near complete. The remainder consists of numerous torsos and a few heads. The figurines are stylized and are reduced to the basic essentials: the legs are rendered as unarticulated stumps, the facial features are indicated by punctures, incisions and applied pellets, and the planes of the faces and torsos are simplified, with no attempt at musculature or naturalistic detail. While the figurines are too crude and stylistically homogeneous to warrant stylistic classification, the differences among them indicate the attempt to depict different kinds of animals. Most of the figurines are either too poorly preserved or too summarily treated to permit positive identification and must simply be classed as bovids. Nevertheless, more specific identifications can be suggested for several examples.

Equids: (9 examples: SI 2 75, 77; SLK 67-295, 565, 642, 936, 958, 1109, WRD 67-45 [Pls. 23-24])

The heads of six stylistically heterogeneous equid figurines were discovered. Though they are probably horses, the possibility that they are donkeys cannot be absolutely ruled out.[38] Their necks are slender, their muzzles are elongated and their manes are prominent. Their eyes consist of either applied pellets with an inner impressed circle and central puncture (SI 2 77 [Pl. 23:1]; SLK 67-936 [Pl. 24:1]) or punctures in the clay (SI 2 75 [Pl. 23:2]). The nostrils are indicated by two punctures in the clay and the mouth is indicated by incised lines (SI 2 75, 77; SLK 67-295, 936). Two of the figurines wear bridles. The bridle of SLK

---

[38] While the slender necks and elongated muzzles support their identification as horses, the treatment of the manes of two of the figurines supports their identification as donkeys since they are erect rather than falling. The prominence of the mane of SI 2 77 and the diagonal grooving of SI 2 75 suggests that they are erect. The history of the horse and the donkey in the Near East, and the artistic representations of equids discovered there do not conclusively argue for the identification of these figurines. Horses do not appear to have become prominent before the Ur III period, but none of the horse figurines from Selenkahiye antedate the Ur III levels. Since Pierre Ducos has cogently argued against the domestication of the onager in Mesopotamia ("The Oriental Institute Excavations at Mureybit, Syria: Preliminary Report on the 1965 Campaign: Part IV: Les restes d'Equidés," *JNES* 29 (1970), pp. 273-289) the equid figurines are either horses or donkeys.

67-936 (Pl. 24:1) consists of strips of clay applied longitudinally to the top of the muzzle, to each side of the bottom of the muzzle and transversely around the outer edge of the muzzle and over the top of the head. The bridle of SLK 67-295 (Pl. 24:2)[39] is indicated by a hole in the side of the muzzle through which reins of another material must have passed. SLK 67-958 and WRD 67-45, both of which are less well preserved, are most likely also horse figurines.

SLK 67-565 and 642 are peculiar figurines which probably represent horses with blinkers, though these figurines differ considerably from the horses discussed above. The best preserved example of this type, SLK 67-642 (Pl. 24:4) has a horizontally grooved applied band which descends from the crown of the head to the broken edge of the muzzle, and a band of clay applied to each side of the head, below the eyes. These latter bands parallel somewhat those of SLK 67-936, and are perhaps best construed as a bridle. A flap of clay extends upward from each of the lateral flaps, covers each of the eyes of the figurine and apparently represents blinkers. A short "mane" extends from the middle of the head to the nape of the neck. SLK 67-565, though not displaying all of the same details, nor as well preserved, apparently belongs to the same general type. SLK 67-1109 (Pl. 24:5) and 1166 (Pl. 23:4) may also be equids.

Donkeys:

The torso and neck of one headless figurine (SLK 67-542 [Pl. 27:1]) with the general configuration of a horse is decorated with vertically incised lines on the front and sides of the neck. Another animal figurine, possibly a donkey, with vertical incisions on its long neck, and which bore a rider, was found during the 1974 season at Seleyahiye.[40] The similarity between the riderless figurine discovered in 1967 and the figurine discovered in 1974 suggests that the riderless figurine may also be a donkey.

Bulls: (9 examples: SI IB 24, 52, SI 2 102, SLK 67-52, 152, 227, 233, 277, 503)

SI IB 24, 52 (Pl. 25:9); SI 2 1-2; SLK 67-52, 152, 227, 277, 427, and 503 (Pl. 25:4),[41] with long, crescent-shaped horns extended sideways and pointing upward, probably represent bulls. The faces of SI IB 24, 52; SI 2 102 and SLK 67-503 (Pl. 25:1-4) are missing. The face of SLK 67-152 (Pl. 25:5) is lacking in detail, and the face of SLK 67-227 (Pl. 25:6), whose muzzle is broken away, has eyes of applied and punctured pellets. SLK 67-427 (Pl. 26:1), the figurine with the best preserved face, but which looks least like a bull, has eyes of dotted circles, nostrils rendered by two punctures in the clay at the thick, blunt end of the muzzle and a mouth rendered by an incised line. WRD 67-44 and SLK 67-233, whose muzzle and horn extremities are broken away may also be bulls. Another, originally long-horned figurine (SLK 67-216 [Pl. 25:7]), whose horns are broken away, and which has an elongated muzzle, may not be a bull.

---

[39] Note that the eyes of this figurine are also rendered by the perforation technique.
[40] Written communication, Maurits van Loon, July 20, 1974.
[41] The horns of S. Surf 155 are broken away, but the remaining stumps suggest that they were prominent and that they probably extended sideways.

2. Classification

Goat: (1 example: SLK 67-352; cf. 500, 1243)

SLK 67-352 (Pl. 26:4) appears to represent a goat. The figurine has partially broken horns which project backward, eyes and nostrils rendered by punctures in the clay, and a grooved mouth. The front of the neck is decorated with incised chevrons, and the top of the head is decorated with two incisions which converge to form a V shape. SLK 67-500, which is rather similar in stature to SLK 67-352, may also be a goat, but the absence of facial features makes a more positive identification difficult. SLK 67-1243 may possibly also be a goat.

Sheep:

One bovid figurine (SLK 67-256 [Pl. 27:2]), with a short stubby neck may represent a sheep. A herringbone pattern is incised on its back and on each of its sides. The front of the figurine is decorated with a series of irregularly incised vertical lines. The incised decorations which cover the figurine may represent a stylized treatment of the animal's coat.[42]

The head of another animal figurine, SLK 67-502 (Pl. 27:3), whose thick horns are missing, may represent the head of a ram. The eyes and nostrils are rendered by punctures in the clay and the mouth by a short, deep incision.

Birds: (14 examples: SLK 67-14, 15, 68, 460, 668, 698, 699, 972, 976, 982, 1110, 1180, 1189, 1512 [Pls. 28-30])

Bird figurines were also found. The best preserved example, SLK 67-68 (Pl. 28:1), is a headless figurine with extended wings and a pinched tail. The figurine, which stands on a relatively tall pedestal that splays at the base, slants upward and gives the impression of a bird in flight.[43] Another headless bird figurine, SLK 67-668 (Pl. 29:1), is similar, but lacks wings. Yet another headless bird figurine (SLK 67-460 [Pl. 29:3]) is crudely incised with non-symmetrical designs which represent the bird's wings, and still another headless bird

---

[42] The use of geometric patterns to render the animal's coat is encountered on a carved stone basin at Tell Mardikh, Giorgio Castellino, *et al.*, *Missione Archeologica Italiana in Siria: Rapporto preliminare della campagna 1965 (Tell Mardikh)*, (Rome, 1966), pl. XIIV, and on Cappodocian cylinder seals, Edith Porada, ed., *Corpus of Ancient Near Eastern Seals in North American Collections* I (New York, 1948), pls. CXXVII-CXXIX. The coat of one of the animals on the Tell Mardikh basin is indicated by a herringbone pattern.

[43] A bird figurine standing on a concave pedestal base was found in phase IV (late third millennium?) at Harran (Kay Prag, "The 1959 Deep Sounding at Harran in Turkey," *Levant* 2 [1970], Fig. 9.78 and Pl. XXXVB). For references to a bird figurine from Mari and a rattle from Brak see Prag, *ibid.*, p. 87. For a rattle in the shape of a bird on a pedestal from Tell Asmar see Henri Frankfort, Seton Lloyd and Thorkild Jacobsen, *The Gimilsin Temple and the Palace of the Rulers at Tell Asmar*, OIP XLIII (Chicago, 1940), Fig. 120 a, b, p. 228. Bird figurines on pedestals are found at a number of sites in the subsequent MB II period. Birds with extended wings and with incised lines across the back and wings were found in Hama H5 (E. Fugmann, *Hama: Fouilles et recherches 1931-1938 II: L'architecture des périodes pré-hellénistiques* [Copenhagen, 1958], Field No. 3 A 34, Fig. 109, p. 89) and in the MB II levels at Nahariya (Ben-Dor, "A Middle Bronze-Age Temple at Nahariyah," *Quarterly of the Department of Antiquities of Palestine* 14 [1950], pl. XII: 10a, b). The birds from both sites are very similar, differing only in the slightly longer neck

figurine (SLK 67-1180), is decorated with punctuate dots. Additional fragments (SLK 67-15 [Pl. 29:2], SLK 67-580, 972 and 976 [Pl. 28:3])[44] apparently also represent birds on pedestals.

Two headless figurines, (SLK 67-698 [Pl. 30:1] and 699 [Pl. 28:2]), standing on narrow pedestals, probably also represent birds. They are decorated with bands of incised parallel lines between which are a series of dots. These bands appear schematically to outline the folded wings of a bird.[45]

Bovids

The remainder of the quadrupeds, which actually constitute the majority of the animal figurines, are either too fragmentary or too generalized to permit a more specific designation. Yet, one particular example, SLK 67-289, is noteworthy. This figurine has centrally punctured applied pellet ears, punctuate dot eyes and nostrils, and a short horizontally grooved mouth. The unusual features are the three prominent grooves on the top of the head and the flap of skin descending the front of the neck.

2.3. Animal and Rider Figurines

(27 examples: SI IB 57; SLK 67-164, 206, 443, 448, 475, 510, 512, 550, 592, 683, 685, 878, 886, 895, 900, 921, 928, 934, 943, 955, 1001, 1025, 1126, 1160, 1164, 1165 [Pls. 28, 30, 30A])

The figurines of this type sit side-saddle on equids identifiable as donkeys.[46] Most of the upper parts of four of the human figurines (SLK 67-592, 683, 685, 955 [Pl. 28:4-7]) are missing. SLK 67-895 (Pl. 30:2) is relatively well preserved, although the head of the rider and the legs of the animal are missing. The human figurine of this composite type is consistently summarily treated and the legs are not rendered. The pillar-shaped rider rises from the animal's back as a forward leaning hump. SLK 67-895 (Pl. 30:2) broadens slightly at the shoulders. The figurine reaches past the donkey's mane with its extended left arm and "hand" while its diminutive right arm-stump extends sideways in the other direction. On the basis of this stylistic detail, several additional figurines whose arms are

---

on the Nahariyah examples and in the taller, splaying pedestal on the Hama example. Whereas the Nahariyah birds have peg holes for attachment to some object, the Hama bird, like the Selenkahiye birds with splaying pedestal bases, were designed to stand. For examples of birds of this type without incisions see Ben-Dor, *ibid.*, pl. XI:21, 25, 26. Additional examples of birds with extended wings but lacking incisions come from Megiddo X (Gordon Loud, *Megiddo II: Seasons of 1935-39*, OIP LXII [Chicago, 1948], pl. 245:18) and Byblos, Deposit 7852-7903 (M. Dunand, *Byblos II*, pl. LV, No. 7896).

[44] SLK 67-15 and 976 are slightly hollow.

[45] Cf. the bird from Harran, (above, n. 43) which has incised decorations on its back and sides.

[46] The side-saddle position and the long ears of one of the equids (SLK 67-895) supports this attribution. Cf. van Loon, *op. cit.* (above, n. 11), p. 29. SI IB 57, with roughly oval-shaped remains of clay attached to its back, probably represents another example of the type. The broken edges represent the places on each side of the animal's back where the rider was smooth-pressed onto the back of the animal.

treated in a similar manner, yet who are presumably broken away from the animals, may be tentatively identified as rider figurines. For example, while only the upper part of SLK 67-1164 (Pl. 30A:1) is preserved, this simplified figurine with prominent eyes and a short ponytail is apparently part of an animal and rider figurine. In some instances the identification of a figurine as belonging to the animal and rider class is based upon the presence of vestiges of riders which remain attached to either the backs or the sides of the animals (i.e., SLK 67-206), or is based upon the peculiar way in which the upper surfaces of the animals are broken away (i.e., SLK 67-512). The rider on SLK 67-206 (Pl. 30:3) is almost completely broken away. Only traces of the side-saddle figure remain, yet this figurine undoubtedly belongs to the class of animal and rider figurines. On the other hand, the dorsal surface of SLK 67-512 is broken away, while two extraneous broken lumps of clay remain applied to one side of the animal. Hence, one has reason to suspect that additional animal figurines with the upper surface and the back broken away may represent animal and rider figurines.

The head type of the rider figurines can be identified on the basis of a well preserved animal and rider figurine found buried beneath the floor of a room during the 1972 excavation at Tell Selenkahiye. The figure, seated sideways on a donkey, grasping the animal's mane with his extended right hand and originally holding some object in his perforated left fist, wears a pointed cap.[47] Presumably, the mounted figurines discovered in 1967 also wore pointed caps. In this detail, they are similar to the male figurines, Type V, who also wear conical shaped headdresses.

The animals, like the riders, are summarily treated. Facial details are lacking and only the manes are rendered. The upper part of the necks and the heads of only two of the animals are preserved (SLK 67-592 [Pl. 28:4] and 895 [Pl. 30:2]). The manes of each of them extend only half way down the neck, but a prominent mane extends to the base of the neck of another figurine missing its head and most of its neck (SLK 67-955 [Pl. 28:7]). While the rider on S1 1B 57 is broken away, traces of the attachment of the rider to the animal remains.

2.4. Model Wagons and Chariots

Fragments of thirty-two wheeled vehicles and numerous wheels were discovered during the 1965 and 1967 seasons at Selenkahiye and Wreyde. Because of the fragmentary nature of the assemblage it is difficult to divide the assemblage into distinct typological groups. In most instances, only the floor and parts of the walls, or corners of the floor and walls are preserved. The floor and superstructure of only one wagon (SLK 67-980 [Pl. 31:1]) is preserved. Nevertheless, the assemblage can be divided into two categories: 1) wagons (four-wheeled vehicles) and 2) chariots (two-wheeled vehicles).[48] While it is sometimes very

---

[47] Maurits van Loon, "First Results of the 1972 Excavations at Tell Selenkahiye," *Annales Archéologiques Arabes Syriennes* XXIII (1973), Fig. 8.

[48] SLK 67-953 may also be a chariot.

difficult to distinguish between the types because of the fragmentary nature of the finds, wagons numerically prevail.[49]

With the exception of SLK 67-953 (Pl. 31:4) both the chariots and wagons are rectangular, with the sides clearly longer than the widths. The floors and the walls are normally modelled from one piece of clay with no attempt to distinguish the floor from the undercarriage. In general, the treatment is summary. When preserved, the front ends are generally pierced for the attachment of the draught poles (SLK 67-35, 669 [Pl. 31:3]), 873, and 980 (Pl. 31:1). SLK 67-894 (Pl. 32:1) features a variant form of attachment to the draught animals. This wagon, whose four walls are missing, has a horizontally perforated projection at the front end of the base.

The axle housings, which are consistently pierced for the admittance of the axle, are rendered in one of three ways: either as a protuberance projecting from the floor of the chariot and horizontally pierced (SLK 67-26, 87, 177, 286, 980 [Pl. 31:1]); as applied and pierced tubular strips of clay (SLK 67-33, 567, 894 [Pl. 32:1-2]); or as horizontal holes pierced in the lower corners of the box (SLK 67-395, 396, 873 [Pl. 32:3]).

While the superstructures of only a few of the vehicles are preserved, they display a fairly wide variety of types. The wagon with the relatively well preserved superstructure (SLK 67-980 [Pl. 31:1]) is open in front, but covered at the rear, forming a seat. The front wall of the wagon, which is broken at the top, is higher than the side and rear walls. While the top of the front wall may have been flat, as the front wall of a rather similar wagon,[50] it probably had a more complex shape, perhaps similar to a terra-cotta wagon in the J. Bomford Collection (England)[51] with a high front wall and covered at the rear. On the basis of the wagon from the Bomford Collection and on the basis of the several metal model wagons from Syria and Anatolia, it seems possible that the top flared out and formed a double arch with or without apertures near the top of each arch. Indeed, three chariot fragments from Selenkahiye, with well preserved front ends, SLK 67-35 (Pl. 33:1), 145 and 354 (Pl. 33:2) are not flat at the top of the front wall. The three broken vertical projections on SLK 67-35 (Pl. 33:1) and SLK 67-145 (Pl. 32:4) probably converged to form two arches with apertures in each, through which the reins passed, while SLK 67-354 is fish-tail shaped.

As noted above, chariots, or perhaps more accurately, carts, are poorly represented in the Selenkahiye assemblage, though they are well represented in Mesopotamian relief and terra-cotta models. SLK 67-354 (Pl. 33:2) with a "fish-tail" flare at the top is probably a chariot, since it accords in shape with two-wheeled chariots from Mesopotamia.[52] One peculiar terra-cotta object with four, tall, out-flaring walls, SLK 67-953 (Pl. 31:4), may represent a two-wheeled chariot, but its axle housing is missing. SLK 67-33 and 1248 also appear to be chariots.

---

[49] For a summary of the representations and terra-cotta models of four-wheeled wagons, see Mary A. Littauer and Joost H. Crouwel, "Early Metal Wagons from the Levant," *Levant* V (1973), pl. SLIV B, pp. 108, 109.

[50] Anton Moortgat, "Tell Chuera: Vorläufiger Bericht über eine Grabungskampagne der M. Frhr. von Oppenhein-Stiftung in Nordmesopotamien 1958," *AAS* 9 (1959), pl. 28.

[51] Littauer and Crouwel, *op. cit.* (above, n. 49). See also the chariot from Hama H6, Fugmann, *op. cit.* (above, n. 43), 5A 602, Fig. 139, p. 111.

[52] See the two-wheeled Sumerian chariot from Kish (ca. 2800-2700 B.C.) (E. Mackay, *A Sumerian Palace and the "A" Cemetery at Kish II* [Chicago 1929], p. 211, Fig. 6, pl. XLVI) and the terra-cotta two-wheeled model chariot from Telloh (A. Parrot, *Tello* (Paris, 1948), p. 264, Fig. 53). Note, however, that the Selenkahiye example lacks the rein apertures found near the top in the Mesopotamian examples.

Approximately half of the wagons[53] are decorated with incised geometric motifs including parallel diagonal lines, longitudinal lines alternating with transverse lines, herringbone patterns,[54] stars, cross-hatching with narrow vertical bands and parallel diagonal lines. One particularly well-decorated chariot, WRD 67-3 (Pl. 34:1) is incised with a herringbone pattern placed between two parallel lines tangent to a series of triangles, the alternate ones being filled with dots. Traces of bitumen are crudely "painted" over parts of the incised decoration of SLK 67-894 (Pl. 32:1). SLK 67-145 (Pl. 32:4) is incised with parallel lines set within contiguous triangles. The decorations are limited to the outside of the vehicle, the inside being left unadorned and in some cases not even smoothed.

Differences in the sub-types of wagons do not appear to accord with differences in decoration. The tendency to incise the wagons is not linked with any other characteristic.

---

[53] SLK 67-26, 43, 145, 177, 395, 396, 544, 672, 867, 873, 894, 993, 1158, 1177, WRD 67-3, 396, (495 and 953 may not be chariots).

[54] As opposed to the wide variety of decorative incisions on wagons discovered in the 1965 and 1967 seasons, the covered wagons discovered during the 1974 season are regularly incised with herringbone patterns.

CHAPTER 3

STRATIGRAPHY AND STYLE

The stratigraphic evidence does not permit establishment of a discernable chronological progression for the Type I and Type V figurines. Indeed, the most prevalent types, I (with the upper arms following the contour of the torso and the attenuated forearms placed across the chest) and V (with arm-stumps extended in front of the body and with conical headdress), appear early in the sequence and continue basically unchanged, in increasing numbers, until the end of the period of occupation. Early examples of Type I include SLK 67-390 (Phase II), SLK 67-1125, 1167, and 1168 (Phase II-III) and SLK 67-606, 684, and 1082 (Phase III). Early examples of Type V include SLK 67-980 and 1085 (Phase II-III) and SLK 67-704 (Phase III). The style appears full-blown and continues unchanged, except for the introduction of several new head types near the end of the sequence. Whereas Types IA (SLK 67-605, 684, and 1082, Phase III), ID (SLK 67-607, Phase III), IF (SLK 67-1181, Phase II-III), IG (SLK 67-945, Phase II-III), and IH (SLK 68-1027, Phase II-III) begin early in the sequence, the stratigraphic evidence does not support an early origin for Types IB and IC, and the earliest Type IE figurine comes from Phase IV (SLK 67-952).

Type III, (with incisions on the shoulder and chest to indicate hair), represented by only one example (SLK 67-391), is found in a Phase II context (Square 26, Level 4, Area 1) and is contemporary with the earliest example of Type I (SLK 67-390) and perhaps slightly earlier than the earliest examples of Type V.

The remaining types: II (figurines whose arms curve upward across the chest); VI (with pointed arm-stumps outstretched sideways); VII (with tall pronged crowns); VIII (a heterogeneous group with cylindrical headdresses); IX (with eyes rendered by punctures in the clay and with crescent-shaped headdress); and animal rider figurines appear late in the sequence. Though one Type II example (SLK 67-666) was found in a Phase IV context, it still postdates the earlier Type III and V examples.

Equids all come from upper levels. Bulls with crescentic horns appear to also come from the upper levels. However, more schematized and less detailed animal figurines generally come from earlier levels. The birds come primarily from Phases IV and V (with the two more stylized birds coming from Phase IV). One bird, however, (SLK 67-260) from Square Q26, Level 2, Area 7 is stratigraphically datable to Phase II.

The model chariot body fragments and the model chariot wheels come predominantly from Phase II-IV. Five wheels come from Phase II-III (SLK 67-667, 947, 951, 1018, 1120) and five come from Phase IV (SLK 67-923, 1043, 1116, 1247, 1326). The ratio changes somewhat regarding the model chariot bodies; twelve from V, three from IV and one from II-III. However, basically the chariots seem to be contemporary with the Type I and III, a few examples coming from Phases II-III, several more from IV and the majority from Phase V.

CHAPTER 4

THE REGIONAL CHARACTER OF THE HUMAN FIGURINES

The figurine types found at Selenkahiye are common to the upper Euphrates Valley. Examples similar in technique and style to those from Selenkahiye have been found at nearby Wreyde, Tel Hadidi, and at Habuba Kabira, north of Selenkahiye. Related figurines have also been found at Tell Freyy[55] and Tell es-Sweyhat.[56] Figurines from Habuba Kabira paralleling those from Selenkahiye include a male head with a conical headdress,[57] and the upper part of the torso of another male figurine with arm stumps extending in front of the body,[58] which accord with Selenkahiye Type V: the upper part of a torso[59] which accords with Selenkahiye Type I; a head[60] which accords with Selenkahiye Type IA and another head[61] which recalls SLK 67-525 (Type IB) (except that the short tresses of the Selenkahiye example are replaced with pincurls in the Habuba Kabira example); and yet another head[62] which accords with SLK 67-1181 (Type IF).

Yet the stylistic repertoires of the Selenkahiye and Habuba Kabira figurines differ somewhat, since several types represented at Selenkahiye are not represented at Habuba Kabira (or at least have not as yet been published), while other types, including an example of a seated figure found at Habuba Kabira,[63] are not represented at Selenkahiye.

The same may be said for the parallels between figurines from Selenkahiye and Tell es-Sweyhat. In addition to similarities in the overall style of figurines from both sites, specific types identified at Selenkahiye are paralleled at Tell es-Sweyhat.[64] Yet a headtype which is rare at Selenkahiye is well represented at Tell es-Sweyhat,[65] and, on the other hand, the "Siamese Twin" figurine represented at Tell es-Sweyhat[66] is not present among the 1965-67 finds from Selenkahiye.[66a] Nevertheless, it is clear that the figurines from these

---

[55] I wish to thank Professor Jim Roberts for allowing me to see unpublished photos of the figurines from the first season.

[56] T.A. Holland, "Preliminary Report on Excavations at Tell es-Sweyhat, Syria, 1973-4," *Levant* 8 (1976), Fig. 15:2-7, 9-14.

[57] *MDOG* 101 (1969), Fig. 22, p. 61.

[58] *Ibid.*, Fig. 23a, p. 62.

[59] *Ibid.*, Fig. 21b, p. 60.

[60] *Ibid.*, Fig. 21a, p. 60.

[61] *MDOG* 102 (1970), Fig. 16, pp. 55.

[62] *Ibid.*, Fig. 15, p. 50.

[63] *Ibid.*, Fig. 13, p. 52.

[64] For example, Type I is paralleled by torsos illustrated in Holland, *op. cit.*, (above, n. 56) by Fig. 15:11, 13 and Type V is paralleled by Fig. 15:5.

[65] Type IG at Selenkahiye is represented by one example, SLK 67-945. Yet, cf. Holland, *op. cit.*, (above, n. 56 by Fig. 15:7, 10, 12).

[66] *Ibid.*, Fig. 15:9.

[66a] A few "Siamese Twin" fragments turned up during the 1972-75 seasons. —The Editor.

sites in the northern Euphrates valley represent a definite regional style.[66b]

How far north and south along the Euphrates are figurines rendered in this regional style found? The upper part of a figurine from the northern site of Til Barsip, with contiguous frontally pierced pellets applied to the sides of the head,[67] parallels a Type ID figurine from Selenkahiye.[68] The Til Barsip example is one of the two published figurines from the site and could conceivably represent an import, but it is more likely to have been locally made.

The southern limits for the style are more difficult to determine since the area between Selenkahiye and Mari is not archaeologically well known. Figurines with perforated ear-flaps, somewhat similar to Selenkahiye Type ID figurines, were found at Mari,[69] but the similarity is only superficial. Furthermore, the figurines from Mari are homogeneous and are superficially similar to only one rare figurine type from Selenkahiye. The Mari figurine assemblage appear to represent an independent tradition.

The Akkadian and Ur III terra-cotta figurines from southern Mesopotamia, i.e., Tell Asmar, differ from those from the Euphrates valley region.[70] While several figurines from Nippur[71] differ from those from Tell Asmar, since their arms are not outspread, and superficially accord with the figurines from Selenkahiye, they nevertheless represent a basically different tradition. Like the figurines from Selenkahiye, the examples from Nippur stand with their arms brought across the chest, the fingers of the hands are indicated by incisions in the clay and in a number of instances they have incisions across the wrists.[72] However, there are distinct differences. Whereas the upper parts of the Selenkahiye figurines are "V" shaped and the lower parts pillar shaped, the upper parts of the Nippur figurines are "A" shaped and their legs taper. Furthermore, while the forearms of the Selenkahiye figurines are either absent or diminutive, the forearms of the Nippur examples are more prominent than the upper arms; while the necklaces of the Selenkahiye figurines are applied and frequently of multiple strands, the necklaces of the Nippur figurines are incised and are of single strands; while the plain torsos of the Selenkahiye figurines suggest that the figurines are fully clothed, or at least deemphasize the notion of sexuality, the pubic triangles of the Nippur figurines are prominently rendered by incision and strippling; while the eyes of the Selenkahiye figurines normally consist of applied and punctured pellets, or

---

[66b] See also the recently published assemblage of figurines found at Tell Hadidi (Rudolph H. Dornemann, "Tell Hadidi: A Millennium of Bronze Age City Occupation," in *Archaeological Reports from the Tabga Dam Project, Euphrates Valley, Syria*, David Noel Freedman Ed., *AASOR* 44, Cambridge, Ma., 1979, p. 117 and Fig. 6).

[67] F. Thureau-Dangin & M. Dunand, *Til Barsib*, pl. XXXIII:25. This figurine comes from a context simply said by the author to probably antedate the Assyrian conquest of 856 B.C. (pp. 94, 95). However, the figurine can be stylistically dated to the end of the third millennium.

[68] SLK 67-438.

[69] Andre Parrot, *MAM I: Le Temple d'Ishtar* (Paris, 1956), pl. LXVIII: 50, 440, 977; *MAM II: Le Palais, Documents et Monuments*, (Paris, 1959), pl. XXVIII: 746, *MAM III: Les Temples d'Ishtarat et de Ninni-zaza*, (Paris, 1967), pl. LXXVIII: 2766. The figurines, which were not found *in situ*, were originally given a pre-Sargonic date by Parrot, but were subsequently given a Sargonic-Isin-Larsa range (*MAM III: Les Temples l'Ishtarat et de Ninni-zaza*, p. 81).

[70] Terra-cotta figurines from the Early Dynastic period are poorly represented. For characteristic southern Mesopotamian terra-cotta female figurines, see Frankfort, Lloyd and Jacobson, *op. cit.* (above n. 43), Figs. 108, 109, p. 221, cf. Frankfort's discussion on pp. 206, 207.

[71] Donald E. McCown, *et. al.*, *Nippur I: Temple of Enlil, Scribal Quarters and Soundings*, OIP LXXVIII (Chicago, 1967), pl. 122:1-3.

[72] Leon Legrain, *Terra-cottas from Nippur* (Philadelphia, 1930), pl. II:7, 10, 11; pl. III:18.

4. The Regional Character of the Human Figurines

applied and punctured pellets with inner impressed circle and a central puncture, the eyes of the Nippur figurines consist of applied, non-punctured pellets. Finally, whereas the headgear and coiffure of the Nippur examples are disproportionately large,[73] the headgear and the coiffure of the Selenkahiye figurines are properly proportioned. Thus the figurines from southern Mesopotamia represent a radically different tradition from those found in sites along the northern Euphrates valley. Til Barsip appears to represent the most northerly limit for the types of figurines which had their center in the bend of the Euphrates east of Aleppo around Selenkahiye. This school of terra-cotta sculpture does not seem to have extended as far south as Mari and certainly did not extend into southern Mesopotamia.

Several isolated examples of figurines similar to those from Selenkahiye have been found west and east of the Euphrates valley. To what extent do these figurines reflect the westward and eastward presence of the northern Euphrates valley school of terra-cotta sculpture? The upper part of a female figurine similar to Selenkahiye Type IX was found in Leve XIV at Byblos.[74] However, this figurine differs from the other figurines from Byblos,[75] which represent a more naturalistic tradition. Therefore, the Byblos example probably represents an import.

The head of a female figurine similar to Selenkahiye Type IA was found in Trench III at Tell Masin.[76] However, this is also an isolated case, since the example differs from the MB I figurines characteristic of Tell Masin and other sites in the Orontes valley. Conversely, the figurines characteristic of the Orontes valley are not found at the northern Euphrates valley sites. A striking figurine type characteristic of Tell Masin,[77] Hama J,[78] and Qatna,[79] but not found in the upper Euphrates valley, has oblong pellets which surround the face, a quadrilateral protuberance behind the head, eyes rendered by applied and punctured pellets, rounded arms, fingerless hands placed on the chest, disengaged elbows and two joined legs. Another[80] figurine type, perhaps even more characteristic of Hama J, has the upper part of the body represented as an irregular, horizontally oriented oval and the base as a pillar which splays. Some examples occur with arms which are reduced to forearms that are brought either obliquely[81] or horizontally across the chest.[82] Others occur with the arms and hands absent by design.[83] The basic shape of the figurine type is conceptually related to the Type II figurines from Selenkahiye. Yet, for the most part, the treatment of the arms and the heads is very different from that of the Selenkahiye figurines. The figurines represent a related but different tradition. Therefore, it is likely that the example from Tell Masin, which accords with the Selenkahiye style, originated at a Euphrates valley site and

---

[73] *Ibid.*, pl. III:13, 16, pl. IV:20, 21.

[74] M. Dunand, *Fouilles de Byblos I* (Paris, 1937), pl. L:3382.

[75] *Ibid.*, pl. XLVIII-L.

[76] *Berytus* 2 (1935) pl. L:112.

[77] *Berytus* 2 (1935), pl. L:81.

[78] Fugmann, *op. cit.* (above, n. 41), Fig. 64, 3D 483, p. 58; *ibid.*, Fig. 106, 5A 617, p. 82; Ingholt, *Rapport* II, p. 39, n. 1.

[79] A photo of the figurine from Qatna is not published. Cf. Du Mesnil Du Buisson, *Berytus* 2 (1935), pp. 128, 129.

[80] In none of the published examples from excavated sites are the lower parts of the figurines preserved. For a reconstruction of the legs see the complete example in the Louvre (*AO* 6510, Paris, Louvre Museum).

[81] Fugmann, *op. cit.* (above, n. 41), see for example Fig. 64, 3C 689, p. 58.

[82] *Ibid.*, Fig. 74, 3A 742, p. 64.

[83] *Ibid.*, Fig. 64, 3C 594, p. 58.

does not serve as evidence for the production of Euphrates valley figurine types in the Orontes valley.

However, the upper part of a headless male figurine, similar to Selenkahiye Type X, found in the Second Mixed Range in the Amuq[84] may have been locally made and may represent a western extension of the northern Euphrates valley terra-cotta tradition. Whereas in the MB II period the terra-cotta figurines from the Amuq are similar to those of the Orontes valley, i.e., Hama and Tell Mardikh, in the MB I period the figurines—represented only by those from the Second Mixed Range—differ from those from the Orontes valley[85] and show a closer kinship with figurines from the northern Euphrates valley and further east to Harran, Tell Jidle and Tell Chuera.

Partially preserved figurines found east of the Euphrates in a sounding at Harran on the Balikh[86] appear to be related to the figurines characteristic of the northern Euphrates valley. Parallels can also be drawn with figurines from Assur E.[87] Signficant parallels are also found at Tell Chuera situated between the Balikh and the Khabur, slightly south of Harran. Figurines from the so-called "North Temple" and from Trench III parallel the Selenkahiye figures in technique and style. The upward curving arms applied to the V-shaped upper torso fragment on one figure from the North Temple[88] accord well with the Selenkahiye Type II figurines. The upper part of another figurine with upcurving arms and with a very substantial coiffure[89] also recalls Selenkahiye Type II.

The applied necklace punctured with short horizontal dashes on the upper part of another figurine from the North Temple[90] accords well with the single and double strand necklaces characteristic of the Selenkahiye figurines. The folded over ear pellets and the eyes of applied and punctured pellets of this figurine are also characteristic of the Selenkahiye assemblage. The V-shaped torso with the hands applied across the chest on a figurine from Trench III[91] accord well with the Type I figurine. And two additional figurines from Chuera, with insubstantial tresses,[92] accord with Selenkahiye Type IC.

Finally, the transverse hole in the muzzle of the draught animal from the North Trench[93] also accords with an animal figurine from Selenkahiye (SLK 67-295 [Pl. 24:2]).

While the terra-cotta figurines from the Euphrates valley appear to be closer in style to those in the Jazirah than to those from areas west of the Euphrates, the northern Euphrates valley appears to be the home of the figurine styles characteristic of Selenkahiye. The virtual confinement of the Selenkahiye figurine types to the northern Euphrates valley suggests that the Northern Euphrates valley is a culturally distinct region with a terra-cotta figurine tradition differing from the terra-cotta figurine traditions found elsewhere in Syria.

---

[84] R. J. Braidwood & Linda S. Braidwood, *Excavations in the Plains of Antioch I* (Chicago, 1960), Fig. 368:4, p. 467; pl. 50:9 and p. 466.

[85] See the author's *Regionalism in the Art of Syria and Palestine in the Middle Bronze Age*, Ann Arbor, University Microfilm, 1972, pp. 55-58, or at least add this.

[86] Note particularly the headless upper part of a female figurine similar to Selenkahiye Type I (*Levant 2* [1970], Fig. 9:70, p. 88). The headless upper part of another figurine (*ibid.*, Fig. 9:71) is also related to the Selenkahiye assemblage, but the absence of the arms does not permit a more specific identification.

[87] Walter Andrae, *Die Archaischen Ischtar Tempel in Assur* (Leipzig, 1922), pl. 56.

[88] A. Moortgat, *Tell Chuera in Nordost-Syrien: Vorläufiger Bericht uber die Dritte Grabungskampagne, 1960* (Koln, 1962), Abb. 7d.

[89] Moortgat, *Tell Chuera: Vorläufiger Bericht über eine Grabungskampagne der M. Frhr. Von Oppenheim Stiftung in Nordmesopotamien 1958*, Abb. 27.

[90] Moortgat, *op. cit.* (above, n. 88) Abb. 7c.

[91] *Ibid.*, Abb. 12b.

[92] *Ibid.*, Abb. 7e, g.

[93] *Ibid.*, Abb. 12a.

CHAPTER 5

FUNCTION OF THE FIGURINES

It is unlikely that the figurines and model chariots were produced as works of pure art. It is also unlikely that they are toys.[94] They are almost certainly associated with the cultic-magical realm.[95] This suggestion is supported by the discovery at Selenkahiye in 1972 of the ritual burial of three female figurines beneath the floor of one room, and the burial of one male figurine beneath the floor of another room.[96] But, are the human figurines images of gods or worshippers? Conceivably, some types may represent gods, while other types may represent worshippers. If some of the figurines represent gods, as identifiable through their divine attributes, i.e., fists pierced to hold a weapon or other attributes, conical caps, etc., are they cheap replicas of the main cult images[97] of the major gods associated with a presumed state religion (which when found in houses represent a manifestation of private worship), or are they household gods associated with popular religion?[98]

Some of the figurines may represent worshippers who sought by means of sympathetic magic to perpetually stand before their god. Indeed figurines which hold birds or young quadrupeds to be sacrificed are certainly worshippers. But, in the absence of these obvious

---

[94] Although some crude ancient figurines have been identified as toys, it is unlikely that the Selenkahiye figurines are toys. For an example of a human figurine identified as a toy, see William Flinders Petrie, *Objects of Daily Use* (London, 1927), p. 61 and pl. LIII. William C. Hayes considers some of the numerous figurines found in Middle Kingdom Egyptian tombs "merely ornaments or parts of toys" (*The Scepter of Egypt: Part I* [New York, 1953], p. 218). A baked clay horse figurine found in the grave of a small child in the cemetery of the Persepolis Spring was also identified as a toy (Erich F. Schmidt, *Persepolis* II, OIP LXIX [Chicago, 1957], p. 120 and pl. 89:1).

[95] Cf. E. Douglas van Buren, *Clay Figurines of Babylonia and Assyria* (New Haven, 1930), pp. xlviii ff.; James B. Pritchard, *Palestinian Figurines in Relation to Certain Goddesses Known through Literature* (New Haven, 1943), pp. 83-87; Ruth Opificius, *Das altbabylonische Terrakottarelief* (Berlin, 1961), pp. 244, 245.

[96] Van Loon, *op. cit.* (above n. 47), p. 148.

[97] Cf. A. Leo Oppenheim, *Ancient Mesopotamia: Portrait of a Dead Civilization* (Chicago and London, 1964), p. 174. A systematic study of the relationship between the rendering of images of the gods in monumental sculpture and in the minor arts is still awaited. For a possible stone sculpture prototype for terra-cotta female figurines supporting their breasts, see the stone statue of a female figure supporting her breasts found in Assur (W. Andrae, *op. cit.* [above, n. 78], pl. 27, 28b, c).

[98] Van Loon identified one of the female figurines buried under the floor of one of the rooms and the male figurine buried under the floor of another room, found during the 1972 excavations as "house gods" and suggested that all iconographically similar figurines served the same purpose (*op. cit.* [above, n. 47], p. 148). For a discussion of the functions of household gods at Nuzi and their bearing on certain Old Testament passages see Anne E. Draffkorn, "Ilani/Elohim," *Journal of Biblical Literature* LXXVI (1957), pp. 216-224. I wish to thank Professor Samuel Iwry for bringing this article to my attention.

attributes,[99] and in the absence of inscriptions[100] and close parallels to the somewhat more readily identifiable Mesopotamian terra-cotta figurines, positive identification of the Selenkahiye figurines is hampered. Therefore, we must depend upon provenience, attributes, and gesture to attain more specific identification.

Since the figurines discovered during the 1965 and 1967 seasons were found randomly distributed in and around the houses, and since three figurines discovered during the 1972 season had been ritually buried beneath the floors of houses rather than in temple contexts, it is unlikely that these figurines represent worshippers. One would expect the figurines of worshippers to be found in temples rather than in private homes.[101] Moreover, it is more difficult to justify the pious burial of figurines of worshippers than a pious burial of figurines of gods.

With respect to attributes, the matter is less clear. While Mesopotamian figures are usually identified as divinities on the basis of their horned crowns, the Selenkahiye figurines consistently lack this attribute.[102] However, the absence of this attribute need not necessarily signify the non-divinity of the Selenkahiye figurines. While in the Ur III and Isin-Larsa periods gods consistently wear the horned crown, in the Early Dynastic period such consistency is absent.[103] Secondly, the figurines may represent minor deities who do not wear crowns.[104] Moreover, since the pottery from Selenkahiye is Syrian in character and the non-ceramic material grows increasingly Syrian in character from phase to phase, an insistence on Mesopotamian attributes is unjustified.

On the other hand, many Type V figurines appear to have formerly held attributes, which if preserved would have supported identification of these figurines as gods. While the attributes are missing, these figurines can be associated with the genre of Syrian warrior gods on the basis of similarities between the gestures of the Selenkahiye figurines and the gestures of the Syrian warrior gods as will become apparent following the latter part of the discussion of the gestures of the figurines.

Undoubtedly, the Type II figurines, whose arms curve upward across the chest and whose hands are vertically aligned, represent goddesses in breast supporting attitudes. However, the gesture of the numerous Type I figurines is more difficult to identify. Worshippers in Near Eastern art traditionally assume one of two characteristic poses: either they rest their clasped hands on their chest or waist, or they bring one hand across their waist while they raise their other arm with the palm inward.[105] The hands of the Selenkahiye Type I figurines are placed across their chests. While this attitude suggests that these figurines may

---

[99] Cf. the worshipper carrying a kid, being led by a minor god to the enthroned sun god on an Akkadian Seal (Porada, *Corpus*, pl. XXXIX:189) and the worshipper carrying a kid, following a minor god holding a mace on another Akkadian seal (*ibid.*, pl. XXX:197).

[100] Mesopotamian figurines are occasionally inscribed, thereby enabling a specific identification of the object (Van Buren, *op. cit.* [above, n. 95], pp. xlii, xliv).

[101] Henri Frankfort suggests that the wide distribution of figurines in private houses at Tell Asmar and at Assur can be explained by assuming that the figures were given as amulets in return for sacrifices (Frankfort, Lloyd and Jacobsen, *op. cit.* [above, n. 41], p. 210).

[102] One may conceive of the pointed caps on some of the figurines as simplified horned crowns. Yet granted this assumption, it would only account for a small minority of the figurines.

[103] Richard Ellis, *Foundation Deposits in Ancient Mesopotamia* (New Haven and London, 1968), p. 74.

[104] McCown, *op. cit.* (above, n. 71), p. 84.

[105] Interceding goddesses usually stand with both arms raised, palms upward. Cf. S. Langdon, "Gesture in Sumerian and Babylonian Prayer," *Journal of the Royal Asiatic Society* (1919), pp. 531-556.

represent worshippers,[106] this identification is not certain. Usually, the hands of Mesopotamian terra-cotta worshipper figurines are either clasped, or touching.[107] The hands of the Selenkahiye figurines are neither clasped, nor touching. The absence of the clasped hand motif appears to be deliberate. Since the treatment of the hands on the Selenkahiye figurines parallels the treatment of the hands of a number of figurines from Nippur correctly identified as figurines in breast supporting positions,[108] the Selenkahiye Type I figurines may represent the breast supporting goddess rather than the worshipper (particularly since the presence of worshipper figurines is difficult to explain in domestic contexts). However, I am more inclined to identify the gesture of the Type I figurines as the gesture of intercessor or personal protective deities who stand with upraised hands in the presence of major deities.[108a]

Several figurines from Selenkahiye (Type V) stand with their arms bent at the elbows and their short, stylized forearms extended in front of them. The extremities of these arm stumps are frequently vertically perforated and probably originally held either weapons, staffs, or standards. Several bronze figurines representing standing figures with arms bent at the elbows, forearms extended before them, and with vertically perforated fists, some of which still retain their weapons, were found in Syrian sites or were said to come from Syria. Perhaps the earliest metal example featuring this motif is represented by a standing nude male figurine wearing a conical cap from Tell Judeideh.[109] Its forearms are raised to shoulder height and its pierced fists formerly held some objects, probably weapons which are now lost. A later figure from Tell Simiryan,[110] which holds an axe in its extended right hand, is a noteworthy example of the type. Other related figurines, including, among others, the silver male and female figurines from Ugarit, were recently collected and published.[111] A crude bronze figurine with Egyptian affinities from Byblos[112] stands with an axe in its extended right hand and a lance in its extended left hand. Presumably, all of these metal figurines represent warrior gods. The Selenkahiye figurines with extended, perforated arm-stumps apparently derive from these metal prototypes and can also be construed as figurines of warrior gods or goddesses.[112a]

---

[106] Van Loon views the figurines whose hands are placed on their chests as being in gesture "closer to the Mesopotamian worship attitude than to the breast-cupping pose associated with the naked Syrian figurine type." ("First Results of the 1967 Excavations at Tell Selenkahiye," *Annales Archéologiques Arabes Syriennes*, XVII [1967], p. 28).

[107] Frankfort, *op. cit.* (above n. 41), Figs. 124a-c, 125a, b; Charlotte Ziegler, *Die Terrakotten von Warka* (Berlin, 1962), pl. 12:189, 190, 192, 195.

[108] Legrain, *op. cit.* (above, n. 72), pl. I:3, II:7, 8, 10-12.

[108a] While the motif of intercessor gods does not become popular until the Old Babylonian Period (cf. Porada, *Corpus*, pl. XLVIII:315-320, XLIX:321-329), it is found on a fragment of limestone relief dated to the end of the Akkadian period (Anton Moortgat, *The Art of Ancient Mesopotamia: The Classical Art of the Near East*, transl. from German by Judith Filson, London and New York, 1969, pl. 158 and p. 56), and on the stele of Urnammu (Frankfort, *op. cit.* [above, n. 16], pl. 53).

[109] R. J. Braidwood and Linda A. Braidwood, *op. cit.* (above, n. 84), pl. 57.

[110] R. J. Braidwood, "Report on Two Sondages on the Coast of Syria, South of Tartous," *Syria* 21 (1940), pl. XXVI and pp. 212, 213.

[111] Cf. Jeanny Vorys Canby, "The Pedigree of a Syrian Bronze in the Walters Art Gallery, Baltimore, and "Some Stylistic Crosscurrents in the Late Third Millennium B.C.," *Berytus* 17 (1968), pp. 107-122.

[112] Maurice Dunand, *Byblos* II (Paris, 1954), pl. LXI:9145.

[112a] We must consider the possibility that some of the headless Type V figurines are female deities since an intact figurine of this type found in 1972 had a feminine coiffure (van Loon, *op. cit.* [above, n. 47] Fig. 7).

Thus, considering the three criteria—provenience, attribute, and gesture—I suggest that the figurines represent household replicas of major and minor deities. Some, such as the male figurines with conical caps and perforated fists reflect the iconography of the major gods, (i.e., the weather or warrior god), while others, such as the figurines with hands across their chests may represent either fertility goddesses, or personal protective deities who are seen to intercede with the major deities on the monuments of the Akkadian and later periods.

The motif of the animal and rider who sits side-saddle is relatively unique, though it is fairly well represented at Selenkahiye.[113] It is found on a terra-cotta plaque from Ishchali, dating to the Isin-Larsa period, on which a human figure sits side-saddle and cross-legged on a humped bull[114] and on a serpentine seal with a warrior with a shield and a figure seated on an equid,[115] probably a donkey. Since the riders on the Selenkahiye examples sit side-saddle and since the animals have long ears, they are probably donkeys. But who are the riders? Are they human, perhaps royal figures, or are they gods? Figures supported by donkeys on Cappadocian cylinder seals and on a mold found in Kultepe level IB were identified as gods.[116] It is likely that the Selenkahiye riders are also gods, particularly since the example found in 1972 had a perforated fist in which he would have held either a staff or weapon.[117]

It is likely that the animal figurines, few of which can be positively identified, were also associated with the religious realm.[118] But, since they are found in domestic contexts, it is improbable that they represent substitute animal sacrifices. Some of them may either represent tokens or amuletic receipts given in exchange for animal sacrifices or talismanic objects used to insure the fertility of the flocks and herds through sympathetic magic.

It may also be noted that bulls are associated with the Weather god. A Weather god holding a lightning fork is featured on an Old Assyrian seal.[119] The Weather god is frequently featured on the back of a bull on Old Babylonian seals.[120] In the Late Bronze and Iron Ages the motif is frequently found on stelae and *kudurrū*. The lowest register of a *kudurrū* from Susa dated by its inscription to the end of the 14th century features

---

[113] Another example of the type was found during the 1972 season (van Loon *op. cit.* [above, n. 47], Fig. 8).

[114] Henri Frankfort, *The Art and Architecture of the Ancient Orient* (Baltimore, 1963) pl. 59 (C).

[115] E. Douglas van Buren, *The Fauna of Ancient Mesopotamia as Represented in Art* (Rome, 1939), Fig. 36.

[116] Nimet Ozguç, *The Anatolian Group of Cylinder Seal Impressions from Kultepe* (Anakara, 1965), p. 68. I wish to thank Jeanny Vorys Canby of the Walters Art Gallery in Baltimore for bringing this reference to my attention.

[117] Van Loon, *op. cit.* (above, n. 47), p. 148.

[118] Seton Lloyd suggested that while anthropomorphic figurines are associated with the religious realm, animal figurines are probably toys. (*The Art of the Ancient Near East* [New York, 1961], pp. 24, 25). However, there is no evidence to support this distinction.

[119] Porada, *op. cit.* (above, n. 42), pl. CXXVII:850.

[120] *Ibid.*, Pl. LXX:507-512.

5. Function of the Figurines

a double lightning fork (the emblem of the Weather god) upon the back of a bull.[121] The same motif is also found on the lowest register of the twelfth century *kudurrū* of Nebuchadnezzar I.[122] The association of the Weather god with bulls continues into the Neo-Assyrian period. Of the file of seven gods featured on a relief from Maltaya, (not to be confused with Malatya), only the god holding forks of lightning stands upon a bull.[123] Note also the god holding a three-pronged thunderbolt who stands on the back of a bull on a stele dated to the 8th or 7th century.[124] On cylinder seals of the Second Syrian Group, the bull is also associated with the nude goddess who stands upon the bull's back.[125]

Undoubtedly, some of the animals, probably the horses (or onagers)[126] and possibly some of the bulls[127] served as draught animals for the chariots, which also appear to have a cultic function. Though the motif of gods in chariots is rarely represented in Mesopotamian art, it is found on three Akkadian cylinder seals[128] on which the anthropomorphic figures, identified as gods by their horned crowns, drive four-wheeled chariots pulled by winged dragons. The image recalls the Weather god since the rumbling of the heavy four-wheeled chariots is suggestive of thunder.[129] Thus, the chariots may represent the vehicles of transportation for the Weather god or War god. The complete model group probably included a chariot, draught animals and an anthropomorphic rider.

Several birds on pedestals have also been found. Though they cannot be explained as surrogate sacrifices, since they were also discovered in domestic contexts, a cultic

---

[121] James B. Pritchard, *The Ancient Near East in Pictures* (Princeton, 1954), Fig. 521, pp. 176, 311; J. de Morgan, *Mémoires de là Délégation en Perse*, Vol. I (Paris, 1900), pl. 15, pp. 170-172.

[122] Pritchard, *op. cit.* (above, n. 121), Fig. 519, pp. 176, 311; Leonard W. King, *Babylonian Boundary-Stones and Memorial Tablets in the British Museum* (London, 1912), pls. 90, 91, pp. 29-36.

[123] Pritchard, *op. cit.* (above, n. 121), Fig. 537, pp. 181, 315; V. Place, *Ninive et l'Assyrie* Vol. 3 (Paris, 1867), pl. 45 lower.

[124] Pritchard, *op. cit.* (above, n. 121), Fig. 500, p. 170; R. D. Barnett, "Hittite Hieroglyphic Texts at Aleppo," *Iraq* 10 (1948), pl. 19, pp. 122-137.

[125] Porada, *op. cit.* (above, n. 42), pls. CXLII:942, CXLIII:944.

[126] It is generally assumed that while the onager or wild ass served as the draught animal for chariots in the third millennium, horses began to serve that function in the first half of the second millennium. Cf. Yigael Yadin, *The Art of Warfare in Biblical Lands*, Vol. 1 (New York, 1963), pp. 38-39; Wolfram Nagel, *Der Mesopotamische Streitwagen und seine Entwicklung im ostmediterranen Bereich* (Berlin, 1966). Now see Ducos, above, n. 38.

[127] The use of bovids as draught animals for chariots and wagons is represented by texts, representations and metal model wagons. Cf. Littauer and Crouwel, *op. cit.* (above, n. 49), pp. 120, 121. Note that bovids served as the draught animals for all of the Anatolian wagons published there (*ibid.*, pls. XXXIV-XLIII). The draught animals of the Syrian wagons are missing. They may also have been bovids. The use of bovids as draught animals may have been reserved for cultic or religious functions.

[128] Henri Frankfort, *The Art and Architecture of the Ancient Orient* (Baltimore, 1963), pl. 45; *Antiquaries Journal* 14 (1934), pl. XLII:U. 18922; E. Strommenger and M. Hirmer, *5000 Years of the Art of Mesopotamia* (trans. from the German by Christina Haglund, New York 1964), pl. 113, third row. With the exception of these religious motifs, chariot scenes are no longer depicted in Mesopotamian glyptic after the Early Dynastic Period (H. Frankfort, *Cylinder Seals* [London, 1939], p. 248; cf. Littauer and Crouwel, *op. cit.* [above, n. 104], p. 122).

[129] Frankfort, *Art and Architecture*, p. 46. Cf. Frankfort, *Cylinder Seals*, pp. 124, 125. The storm god is also said to travel upon the clouds (Samuel Noah Kramer, *The Sumerians* [Chicago, 1963], p. 117).

connection is probable. Since occasionally birds were offered as sacrifices,[130] perhaps the bird figurines represent some type of amuletic receipt given in exchange for the sacrifices. On the other hand, birds were used in Assyria, Asia Minor, Egypt and Syria-Palestine as oracular animals, with their behavior observed as a source of divination.[131] They may therefore be associated somehow with divination.[132]

---

[130] Birds do not appear to have a particularly dominant role in the sacrificial cult in Mesopotamia (cf. H. W. F. Saggs, *The Greatness that Was Babylon* [New York, 1962], pp. 351-354). Yet, since there was a particular need to prohibit the offering of birds to Chthonian goddesses, the occasional use of bird sacrifices is implied (cf. Oppenheim, *op. cit.* [above, n. 82], p. 191). In the Old Testament birds are used in the establishment of a covenant (Genesis 15:10), as part of purification rites (Leviticus 14:4, 14:14) and as sacrifices offered by the poor (Leviticus 1:14, 5:7, 12:8).

[131] Oppenheim, *op. cit.* (above, n. 82), pp. 209ff. Birds frequently appear in Mesopotamian seals, where birds of prey symbolized some evil being (Frankfort, *Cylinder Seals*, p. 133). However, the attribution of this meaning to the birds from Selenkahiye is unjustified. In the Aegean, birds are associated with the realm of the gods. Gods sometimes appeared in the shape of birds (F. Matz, "The Maturity of Minoan Civilization," *Cambridge Ancient History*, Vol. II, Part I: *History of the Middle East and the Aegean Region c. 1800-1380*, I. E. S. Edwards, C. J. Gadd, N. G. L. Hammond, E. Sollberger, eds., 3rd ed. [Cambridge, 1973], pp. 161, 162; W. K. C. Guthrie, "The Religion and Mythology of the Greeks, *Cambridge Ancient History*, Vol. II, 2nd ed., Ch. XL [Cambridge, 1961], p. 27; Martin P. Nilsson, *A History of Greek Religion*, trans. from the Swedish by F. J. Fielden, 2nd ed. [New York, 1964], pp. 17, 18, 27). However, the attribution of this interpretation to bird figurines in Syria is unwarranted.

[132] As bulls are associated with the Weather god, so are doves associated with the Love goddess on Syrian seals of the earlier second millennium, e.g., Porada, *op. cit.* (above, n. 42), pl. 143:945-946. —The Editor.

CATALOGUE A

TERRA-COTTA HUMAN FIGURINES

REGISTRATION NUMBER	PLATE	SQUARE	AREA	LEVEL	HEIGHT	WIDTH	THICKNESS	DESCRIPTION
S. Surf. 158	–	–	–	0	5.3	2.0	1.8	torso fragment
S. Surf. 159	–	–	–	0	3.4	2.1	1.1	upper body
S. Surf. 160	–	–	–	0	6.5	3.6	1.8	upper body
S. Surf. 163	18:1	–	–	0	4.0	2.2		head
SI 1 5	–	–	6	1	2.9	2.8	1.0	head
SI 1 6	–	–	–	1	5.8	3.0	1.0	upper body
SI 1 30	–	–	4	1B	3.7	2.7	1.7	head
SI 1 31	–	–	–	1	4.8	2.8	1.7	base
SI 1 33	–	–	–	1	4.0	3.5	0.8	upper body
SI 1 36	–	–	7	1	3.0	1.9	1.0	head
SI 1 37	–	–	7	1	3.5	3.2	1.7	base
SI 1 38	–	–	7	1	3.9	2.0	1.1	torso
SI 1 42	–	–	–	1	3.8	3.5	1.4	upper body
SI 1 46	–	–	–	1	4.0	2.8	1.3	upper body
SI 1 47	–	–	–	1	4.8	3.5	1.4	"legs" & base
SI 1 112	–	–	–	1	5.5	2.6	1.2	torso fragment
SI 1 113	–	–	–	1	2.6	2.0	1.0	torso fragment
SI 1 114	–	–	–	1	6.2	3.7	1.4	torso fragment
SI 1 115	–	–	–	1	3.2	2.9	1.0	torso fragment
SI 1 116	–	–	–	1	6.0	2.7	1.5	torso fragment
SI 1 117	–	–	–	1	3.0	2.5	1.1	torso fragment
SI 1B 9	18:2	–	4	1B	3.9	2.5	1.5	head
SI 1B 10	–	–	4	1B		1.4	1.0	head
SI 1B 11	–	–	4	1B	4.8	4.0	1.4	upper body
SI 1B 12	14:4	–	4	1B	3.4	2.5	1.0	upper body
SI 1B 14	16:6	–	4	1B	3.0	2.1	1.1	head
SI 1B 17	–	–	6	1B	2.6	1.7	1.3	head
SI 1B 19	–	–	4	1B	4.2	2.9	1.6	lower body
SI 1B 20	–	–	4	1B	4.5	2.0	1.8	head
SI 1B 21	16:4	–	4	1B	3.1	1.7	1.0	head
SI 1B 23	–	–	–	1B	2.0	2.0	1.3	head
SI 1B 25	–	–	5	1B	2.5	1.5	1.1	head
SI 1B 43	11:5	–	7	1B	3.8	2.7	1.2	upper torso
SI 1B 45	–	–	7	1B	3.8	3.5	2.1	"legs" & base
SI 1B 48	–	–	7	1B	7.8	2.8	1.0	"legs" & base
SI 1B 49	–	–	1	1B	6.0	3.0	1.7	"legs" & base
SI 1B 50	–	–	1	1B	4.5	3.6	1.8	"legs" & base
SI 1B 51	–	–	1	1B	3.6	2.8	2.1	head
SI 1B 53	–	–	1	1B	6.6	4.3	1.6	upper body

REGISTRATION NUMBER	PLATE	SQUARE	AREA	LEVEL	HEIGHT	WIDTH	THICKNESS	DESCRIPTION
SI 1B 54	–	–	1	1B	2.8	2.5	1.9	head
SI 1B 55	–	–	1	1B	4.5	1.2	0.9	lower body
SI 1B 60	–	–	2	1B	3.9	2.8	1.0	lower torso & "legs"
SI 1B 61	18:3	–	1	1B	2.8	1.3	0.9	head
SI 1B 63	13:5	–	1	1B	4.5	3.8	1.2	upper body
SI 1B 64	–	–	1	1B	7.3	3.6	1.6	base
SI 1B 70	–	–	2	1B	4.5	4.5	1.8	upper body
SI 1B 72	–	–	2	1B	4.0	3.6	1.6	base
SI 1B 73	–	–	2	1B	2.7	2.6	1.5	base
SI 1B 74	–	–	1	1B	7.8	4.3	2.0	"legs" & base
SI 1B 83	–	–	3	1B	3.6	2.2	2.0	head
SI 1B 84	–	–	1	1B	3.5	2.7	1.8	base
SI 1B 85	–	–	1	1B	4.9	2.2	1.3	base
SI 1B 86	–	–	1	1B	5.4	3.1	1.1	torso
SI 1B 89	5:4	–	1	1B	4.6	4.6	1.4	shoulders to waist
SI 1B 92	–	–	–	3	5.4	2.5	1.4	head
SI 1B 93	13:6	–	4	1B	8.6	5.1	1.1	torso
SI 1B 95	–	–	1	1B	7.8	4.7	1.1	torso
SI 1B 96	–	–	3	1B	8.8	3.4	2.1	base
SI 1B 97	–	–	2	1B	7.6	3.6	1.8	"legs" & base
SI 1B 98	–	–	2	1B	4.1	3.9	2.7	base
SI 1B 100	–	–	3	1B	4.9	2.8	1.9	body
SI 1B 104	–	–	3	1B	3.8	3.3	1.2	upper body
SI 1B 106	–	–	3	1B	5.6	3.9	1.7	"legs" & base
SI 1B 108	–	–	1	1B	3.2	2.7	1.4	base
SI 1B 109	14:1	–	1	1B	4.3	2.4	1.1	upper body
SI 1B 110	–	–	1	1B	3.6	3.5	1.3	base
SI 1B 125	–	–	7	1B	4.1	3.9	1.3	chest & arm
SI 1B 126	–	–	7	1B	2.5	1.8	0.8	body fragment
SI 1B 127	–	–	7	1B	2.1	1.5	1.4	body fragment
SI 1B 128	–	–	7	1B	2.5	1.0	–	chest/shoulder
SI 1B 129	5:3	–	5	1B	6.1	5.7	0.9	upper body
SI 1B 130	–	–	5	1B	2.3	1.6	1.1	fragment
SI 1B 131	–	–	5	1B	5.2	2.5	1.2	fragment
SI 1B 132	–	–	5	1B	2.5	2.5	1.5	"legs" & base
SI 1B 136	–	–	5	1B	3.3	2.5	1.1	torso fragment
SI 1B 142	–	–	1	1B	4.2	3.4	1.0	fragment
SI 1B 143	–	–	1	1B	5.4	3.1	1.5	base
SI 2 4	–	–	1	2	4.6	2.3	1.1	lower body
SI 2 27	–	–	1	2	4.8	3.6	1.1	neck to torso
SI 2 65	–	–	1	2	4.6	3.2	1.4	base
SI 2 68	21:1	–	1	2	3.2	2.4	1.3	head
SI 2 71	–	–	1	2	5.0	3.7	1.6	base
SI 2 76	21:2	–	1	2	2.6	1.3	1.0	head
SI 2 78	–	–	3	2	6.6	2.8	1.0	"legs" & base
SI 2 79	–	–	1	2	5.8	4.3	3.5	head

A. Terra-Cotta Human Figurines

REGISTRATION NUMBER	PLATE	SQUARE	AREA	LEVEL	HEIGHT	WIDTH	THICKNESS	DESCRIPTION
SI 2 80	–	–	1	2	5.3	4.3	1.1	foot
SI 2 91	–	–	1	2	6.2	2.9	1.1	"legs" & base
SI 2 111	–	–	3	2	7.0	2.2	1.5	torso & "legs"
SI 2 120	–	–	1	2	3.6	1.6	1.0	"legs"
SI 2 121	–	–	1	2	3.5	2.0	1.1	"legs"
SI 3 88	–	–	–	3	3.6	2.8	1.6	upper body
SI 3 92	7A:1	–	–	–				head
SLK 67-1	2:3	–	–	0	4.9	4.8	1.1	bust
SLK 67-2	12:7	–	0		5.7	4.3	1.1	head, bust
SLK 67-3	4:5	–	–	0	5.2	4.4	1.2	upper torso
SLK 67-4	19:3	–	–	0	4.0	1.9	0.2	head
SLK 67-5	–	–	–	0	2.8	2.4	1.0	upper torso fragment
SLK 67-6	–	–	–	0	7.0	4.1	1.5	upper torso fragment
SLK 67-7	–	–	–	0	5.0	4.2	1.6	upper torso fragment
SLK 67-8	–	–	–	0	5.2	2.7	1.4	neck & frag. of head
SLK 67-9	–	–	–	0	–	–	–	base
SLK 67-10	–	–	–	0	6.5	3.2	2.0	base & lower torso
SLK 67-11	11:4	–	–	0	4.4	2.8	1.2	base
SLK 67-12	–	–	–	0	4.2	1.9	1.1	base
SLK 67-13	–	–	–	0	–	–	–	deep concave base
SLK 67-16	–	–	–	0	3.5	3.2	1.6	base
SLK 67-17	–	–	–	0	5.8	2.4	1.0	base
SLK 67-18	–	–	–	0	4.0	3.1	1.1	upper torso fragment, right arm
SLK 67-19	10:2		–	0	3.4	2.5	1.0	upper torso fragment with arms
SLK 67-21	–	–	–	0	3.1	2.6	1.5	torso fragment
SLK 67-23	–	–	–	0	5.1	2.2	0.9	torso fragment
SLK 67-32	–	–	–	0	8.3	2.6	1.0	base
SLK 67-41	–	Q27	4	1	4.1	1.8	1.2	torso fragment with arms
SLK 67-42	2:4	Q27	2	1	5.4	5.1	1.0	bust
SLK 67-45	–	–	–	0	4.5	2.4	1.2	upper torso fragment w/arm stumps
SLK 67-47	–	–	–	0	3.2	2.0	1.0	head
SLK 67-66	–	Q27	9	1	5.4	4.7	1.8	base & torso
SLK 67-67	–	Q27	13	1	8.7	3.3	1.6	base
					4.9	4.9	–	base diameter

REGISTRATION NUMBER	PLATE	SQUARE	AREA	LEVEL	HEIGHT	WIDTH	THICKNESS	DESCRIPTION
SLK 67-70	–	Q27	11	1	7.2	2.5	1.8	base & lower torso
					4.3	2.5	1.8	base diameter
SLK-67-79	10:3	W43	1	3	6.4	4.7	1.6	upper torso with arms
SLK-67-84	–	–	–	0	6.6	2.3	1.0	base
SLK 67-86	–	–	–	0	4.8	2.5	–	torso with one arm
SLK 67-116	4:1	W41	–	4	7.9	4.2	1.5	neck to base
SLK 67-125	2:2	Q26	–	0	6.0	3.9	0.9	head, left shoulder
SLK 67-127	–	Q26	–	0	5.4	3.1	1.0	neck to "legs"
SLK 67-128	–	Q26	–	0	5.9	4.6	1.7	base
SLK 67-130	–	Q26	–	1	3.6	2.2	–	"legs" & base
					3.5	3.5	–	base diameter
SLK 67-131	–	Q26	4	1	2.8	1.5	–	base
SLK 67-132	–	Q26	3	1	4.9	2.0	1.0	"legs" & base
					3.0	2.7	–	base diameter
SLK 67-144	15:3	–	–	0	5.2	4.7	1.1	upper torso fragment
SLK 67-146	3A:1	–	–	0	6.4	4.8	1.0	head to waist
SLK 67-147	–	–	–	0	3.1	1.9	1.5	head
SLK 67-148	–	–	–	0	4.6	3.0	0.8	bust
SLK 67-149	–	–	–	0	5.3	5.1	1.1	torso fragment
SLK 67-150	–	–	–	0	5.5	2.6	0.9	base
SLK 67-151	–	–	–	0	3.7	2.6	1.5	head
SLK 67-154	–	–	–	0	4.4	1.6	–	"legs" & base
SLK 67-155	11:2	–	–	0	9.0	6.4	2.0	base of neck to lower torso
SLK 67-158	–	–	–	0	5.2	2.9	1.0	torso fragment
SLK 67-163	–	–	–	0	5.6	5.0	1.3	shoulders to below waist
SLK 67-167	–	Q26	–	7	3.4	2.4	1.1	"legs" & base
					3.4	3.4	–	base diameter
SLK 67-179	–	–	–	0	3.4	2.4	1.2	upper torso fragment
SLK 67-180	9:3	–	–	0	3.1	2.3	1.2	head
SLK 67-204	–	P26	–	1	4.5	2.1	1.1	base
SLK 67-207	5:1	R26	3	1	4.0	3.2	2.0	head
SLK 67-208	–	R26	3	1	3.9	2.1	1.2	base & neck to "legs"
SLK 67-213	–	R26	4	1	5.3	3.0	0.8	bust
SLK 67-214	17:1	R26	4	1	5.2	3.4	1.1	neck to waist
SLK 67-218	–	X43	–	1	8.4	4.8	1.9	base & neck
SLK 67-236	–	Q26	5	1	4.2	2.1	1.6	base
SLK 67-239	–	Q26	1	1	3.1	1.6	1.5	"legs" & base
					2.3	2.3	–	base diameter

A. Terra-Cotta Human Figurines

REGISTRATION NUMBER	PLATE	SQUARE	AREA	LEVEL	HEIGHT	WIDTH	THICKNESS	DESCRIPTION
SLK 67-240	–	Q26	1	1	5.5	2.3	1.4	"legs" frag.
SLK 67-241	–	Q26	mixed upper loci	2	4.6	2.2	1.1	"legs" & base
					4.0	4.0	–	base diameter
SLK 67-247	–	Q26	2	1	3.2	1.9	1.2	"legs" & base
					2.5	2.5	–	base diameter
SLK 67-249	–	Q26	7	1	4.3	2.4	1.2	base
SLK 67-251	–	R26	1	1	2.3	1.1	1.0	torso fragment
SLK 67-252	–	Q26	2	1	4.8	4.2	1.1	torso fragment
SLK 67-254	–	Q26	7	2	4.5	4.4	1.1	torso fragment
SLK 67-261	–	Q26	2	1	4.2	3.3	1.2	torso fragment
SLK 67-262	16:5	Q26	2	1	3.0	2.0	1.8	head
SLK 67-263	–	X43	1	3	5.3	2.4	1.2	"legs" & base
					3.0	3.0		base diameter
SLK 67-279	–	Q26	7	2	6.0	2.6	1.8	torso fragment
SLK 67-281	–	Q26	7	2	5.0	2.4	1.7	torso fragment
SLK 67-294	15:4	R26	4	1	6.0	2.5	1.3	torso & one arm
SLK 67-298	–	–	–	0	7.7	5.5	1.7	neck to below waist
SLK 67-299	–	–	–	0	6.6	6.1	1.4	neck to lower torso
SLK 67-300	16:3	–	–	0	5.4	3.2	2.4	head
SLK 67-303	–	–	–	0	3.1	2.0	1.2	head & neck
SLK 67-310	–	–	–	0	6.2	6.0	0.8	body
SLK 67-311	–	–	–	0	6.2	3.7	1.7	torso
SLK 67-312	–	–	–	0	7.6	2.4	1.6	square
					3.7	3.7	–	base
SLK 67-313	–	–	–	0	5.3	2.4	2.3	oval legs & base
					4.2	3.4	–	base diameter
SLK 67-314	–	–	–	0	3.5	2.2	1.5	head
SLK 67-315	–	–	–	0	5.5	2.5	1.5	lower torso
SLK 67-323	–	V43	–	4	5.3	2.5	1.4	"legs" & base
					3.2	3.2	–	base diameter
SLK 67-339	–	Q26	14	2	2.8	1.6	–	"legs" & base
					3.1	3.1	–	base diameter
SLK 67-348	–	Q27	12	1	3.8	2.9	1.5	legs
SLK 67-353	–	R26	2	2	4.6	2.7	–	base
SLK 67-378	22:1	V43	–	6	12.3	7.0	3.3	torso fragment
SLK 67-382	7:4	–	–	0	4.6	3.2	2.6	head
SLK 67-390	4:2	P26	1	4	7.2	5.6	1.1	shoulders to "legs" & base
SLK 67-391	12:3	P26	1	4	6.6	3.9	1.5	head to waist
SLK 67-392	7:2	R26	2	2	7.3	4.6	1.1	head to waist
SLK 67-398	–	Y25	–	1	4.0	2.7	2.3	head to neck

REGISTRATION NUMBER	PLATE	SQUARE	AREA	LEVEL	HEIGHT	WIDTH	THICKNESS	DESCRIPTION
SLK 67-399	18:5	near Y25	—	0	4.5	2.0	1.3	head
SLK 67-401	—	near Y25	—	0	3.2	2.8	1.2	torso
SLK 67-404	—	Q27	2	2	—	—	1.5	"legs" & base
					3.3	3.3	—	base diameter
SLK 67-408	—	R26	1	1	3.8	1.8	0.8	base
SLK 67-425	10:1	Y25	E8	1	6.0	4.9	1.1	shoulders to waist
SLK 67-437	—	R26	6	2	4.5	2.1	1.6	"legs" & base
					3.6	3.6	—	base diameter
SLK 67-438	8:3	Y25	M3	1	8.1	4.9	1.3	upper part
SLK 67-441	—	V25	—	1	4.0	2.9	1.5	base
SLK 67-442	19:2	V25	—	1	6.5	3.0	2.6	head
SLK 67-463	—	U25	—	2	8.1	2.1	1.0	torso & base
					3.4	3.4	—	base diameter
SLK 67-464	—	U25	—	1	4.6	3.2	1.4	"legs" & base
					4.8	2.6	—	base dimensions
SLK 67-466	—	U25	—	1	5.1	2.9	1.3	base
SLK 67-467	—	R26	2	1	3.2	2.4	1.1	"legs" & base
					3.8	3.8	—	base diameter
SLK 67-476	2:1	—	—	0	7.7	4.6	1.1	head to waist
SLK 67-477	10:4	—	—	0	5.9	4.5	1.4	neck to waist
SLK 67-478	19:4	—	—	0	6.3	3.3	1.7	head
SLK 67-479	18:6	—	—	0	4.7	2.0	1.9	head
SLK 67-480		—	—	0	6.7	4.9	1.3	torso fragment
SLK 67-481		—	—	0	4.9	4.0	1.1	torso fragment
SLK 67-482		—	—	0	4.3	3.5	1.1	torso fragment
SLK 67-483		—	—	0	3.7	2.6	0.9	torso fragment
SLK 67-484		—	—	0	3.2	3.3	1.1	torso fragment
SLK 67-485		—	—	0	3.6	1.7	1.4	head
SLK 67-486		—	—	0	3.3	2.8	1.2	fragment
SLK 67-487		—	—	0	3.1	2.2	0.8	torso fragment
SLK 67-489	22:2	—	—	0	11.2	3.8	1.0	torso & base
					3.4	3.4	—	base diameter
SLK 67-490		—	—	0	4.4	2.3	1.0	"legs" & base
					2.5	2.5	—	base diameter
SLK 67-491		—	—	0	4.0	2.0	1.0	"legs" & base
					3.0	3.0	—	base diameter
SLK 67-492		—	—	0	5.2	1.9	1.5	base
SLK 67-493	21:7	—	—	0	7.6	2.7	1.3	base
SLK 67-494		—	—	0	3.3	1.9	1.0	"legs" & base
					2.3	2.3	—	base diameter
SLK 67-523		X25	3B2	1	3.5	3.5	3.1	torso fragment
SLK 67-525	6:2	X25	2H7	1	3.9	3.6	3.5	head
SLK 67-526	1:1	X25	4C9	1	11.5	5.5	—	complete figurine
					3.3	3.3	—	base diameter
SLK 67-527		X25	4B9	1	6.3	1.9	1.4	"legs" & base
					3.3	3.3	—	base diameter
SLK 67-531	12:5	X25	4A10	1	7.0	5.0	0.9	head to lower torso
SLK 67-532		X25	2F6	1	5.2	3.6	0.7	neck & torso

A. Terra-Cotta Human Figurines

REGISTRATION NUMBER	PLATE	SQUARE	AREA	LEVEL	HEIGHT	WIDTH	THICKNESS	DESCRIPTION
SLK 67-533		Y25	A1	1	3.7	3.7	1.0	bust, arms missing
SLK 67-534		X25	4D10	1	6.0	2.0	1.1	base
SLK 67-537		X25	2F10	1	3.4	2.0	1.0	"legs" & base
					3.0	3.0	—	base diameter
SLK 67-540		U25	—	1	5.1	1.8	0.9	"legs" & base
					2.9	2.9	—	base diameter
SLK 67-543		U25	—	1	7.4	2.2	1.0	base & lower torso
					2.9	2.9	—	base diameter
SLK 67-545		U25	—	1	3.7	3.1	1.5	neck & torso
SLK 67-547		U25	—	1	7.3	2.8	1.3	"legs" & base
					3.8	2.6	—	base dimensions
SLK 67-548		U25	—	1	6.9	5.6	1.8	torso
SLK 67-549		U25	—	1	5.6	3.1	1.1	"legs" & base
					4.3	4.0		base diameter
SLK 67-550		U25	—	1	6.1	3.9	1.1	neck & torso
SLK 67-551		V25	—	1	5.3	5.0	0.9	neck & torso
SLK 67-552		V25	—	1	7.5	3.2	1.3	"legs" & base
					4.4	8.0	—	base diameter
SLK 67-553		U25	—	1	8.6	8.0	1.9	torso
SLK 67-558		V25	—	1	4.7	4.6	3.3	head
SLK 67-560		V25	—	1	4.5	3.5	0.9	torso
SLK 67-561		V25	—	1	7.0	6.5	2.2	torso
SLK 67-562		V25	—	1	9.0	3.7	1.3	neck to lower torso
SLK 67-564	6:4	U25	—	1	4.5	3.0	1.5	head
SLK 67-565		U25	—	1	8.1	4.5	2.4	head
SLK 67-566		V25	—	1	8.2	5.0	1.5	neck & torso
SLK 67-572		Y24	—	1	8.7	2.3	1.1	base & torso
					3.2	3.2		base diameter
SLK 67-574		X25	4D10	1	4.3	1.9	1.0	"legs" & base
					3.0	3.0	—	base diameter
SLK 67-576		W25	3A2	1	5.9	2.4	1.3	base
SLK 67-577		Y25	M10	1	4.9	1.7	1.4	"legs" & base
					3.0	2.6	—	base diameter
SLK 67-583		W42	—	4	8.0	5.5	1.1	neck to "legs"
SLK 67-585		W25	1	1	3.5	2.1	0.9	"legs" & base
					3.1	3.1	—	base diameter
SLK 67-587		W25	4	1	3.5	2.1	0.9	"legs" & base
					3.1	3.1	—	base diameter
SLK 67-588	3:1	W25	4	1	6.3	6.2	1.3	head to shoulders
SLK 67-591		W25	4	1	4.0	2.3	1.1	base
SLK 67-594		W25	3	1	7.3	3.1	1.5	"legs"
SLK 67-595	5:2	W25	1	1	4.7	3.3	0.9	head & neck
SLK 67-596		W25	3	1	4.7	3.6	1.2	neck to waist
SLK 67-597		W25	3BS	1	4.8	1.6	—	torso fragment
SLK 67-598		W25	1	1	3.9	—	—	head
SLK 67-604	21:5	W42	2	4	8.2	2.1	1.2	"legs" & base

REGISTRATION NUMBER	PLATE	SQUARE	AREA	LEVEL	HEIGHT	WIDTH	THICKNESS	DESCRIPTION
SLK 67-605a		W42	1	4	3.4	3.0	1.4	head
SLK 67-605b		W42	1	4	9.7	3.1	1.1	"legs"
					3.6	3.6	–	base diameter
SLK 67-606a		W42	1	5	5.3	5.2	1.1	torso
		W42	1	5	4.2	2.3	1.2	legs
SLK 67-607	7:1	W42	1	5	7.0	4.8	1.0	bust
SLK 67-609		W42	1	4	6.7	2.5	1.2	body fragment
SLK 67-610		X25	3	1	3.4	1.2	1.2	"legs" & base
					2.9	2.9	–	base diameter
SLK 67-620	18:4	V25	–	1	5.4	2.3	1.1	head
SLK 67-621		V25	–	2	5.9	3.1	2.1	"legs" & base
					5.4	5.4	–	base diameter
SLK 67-623	12:6	V25	–	2	3.1	1.9	1.1	head
SLK 67-629		W25	3	1	4.9	2.1	1.5	torso fragment
SLK 67-632		X24	1	1	6.0	5.2	1.1	neck & torso
SLK 67-633	13:3	X24	1	1	5.7	4.4	1.0	neck to "legs"
SLK 67-634		W24	1	1	7.2	2.6	1.2	"legs" & base
					3.6	3.6	–	base diameter
SLK 67-635	11:1	X24	1	1	7.3	5.9	1.6	shoulder to "legs"
SLK 67-636		W24	1	1	5.8	3.1	1.1	neck to "legs"
SLK 67-638	6:5	X25	–	1	4.0	3.0	1.5	head
SLK 67-639	16:1	X25	–	1	5.7	1.7	1.1	head
SLK 67-640		W24	1	1	4.5	1.8	–	"legs" & base
					3.8	3.8	–	base diameter
SLK 67-644		W24	2	1	4.0	1.8	1.4	"legs" & base
					2.8	2.8	–	base diameter
SLK 67-645		W24	1	1	4.5	3.1	1.5	head
SLK 67-646		W24	2	1	7.3	3.4	1.0	neck to "legs"
SLK 67-647		X25	–	1	6.1	2.0	1.0	"legs" & base
					3.5	3.0	–	base diameter
SLK 67-650		X25	2	1	4.0	2.1	1.1	"legs" & base
					2.6	2.6	–	base diameter
SLK 67-653		W24	2	1	8.8	2.8	1.0	"legs" & base
					3.6	3.6	–	base diameter
SLK 67-656		W24	2	1	5.0	3.3	3.1	head
SLK 67-657		X24	1	1	7.7	2.7	1.1	"legs" & base
					3.4	3.4	–	base diameter
SLK 67-658		W24	2	1	5.0	2.6	1.1	"legs" & base
					3.1	2.0	–	base diameter
SLK 67-662		V25	–	2	4.4	2.3	1.1	"legs" & base
					4.0	3.5	–	base diameter
SLK 67-665		V25	–	2	10.6	5.1	3.0	shoulder to base
SLK 67-666	10:5	V25	–	2	5.6	5.2	1.9	neck to waist
SLK 67-670		V24	–	1	7.5	4.2	2.1	"legs" & base
					4.7	3.0	–	base diameter
SLK 67-673		V24	–	1	7.4	2.6	1.0	"legs" & base
					3.2	2.9	–	base diameter
SLK 67-674		V24	–	1	6.7	3.3	1.3	neck to base
					3.2	3.2	–	base diameter

A. Terra-Cotta Human Figurines

REGISTRATION NUMBER	PLATE	SQUARE	AREA	LEVEL	HEIGHT	WIDTH	THICKNESS	DESCRIPTION
SLK 67-676	6:1	V24	—	1	4.0	3.0	2.8	head
SLK 67-677		V24	—	1	5.5	2.3	1.0	"legs" & base
					3.8	3.6	—	base diameter
SLK 67-679		V24	—	1	4.6	3.8	1.1	torso
SLK 67-680		V24	—	1	4.7	4.6	1.2	torso, arms
SLK 67-681	17:4	V24	—	1	6.3	4.5	—	neck to base
SLK 67-684	1:2	W24	1	5	16.6	5.7	1.0	complete figure
					3.9	3.5	—	base diameter
SLK 67-686		Y25	—	1	5.6	2.3	1.3	"legs" & base
					3.2	3.2	—	base diameter
SLK 67-687		W25	—	1	6.5	5.1	1.2	"legs" & base
					4.3	3.8	—	base diameter
SLK 67-690		W25	2	1	6.0	5.8	1.0	neck to waist
SLK 67-691		W25	—	1	7.4	2.1	1.1	"legs" & base
					3.2	3.2	—	base diameter
SLK 67-692		Y25	—	1	7.8	2.7	0.9	head to waist
SLK 67-694		Y24	—	1	7.7	6.5	1.2	torso
SLK 67-695	12:1	V25	—	2	7.7	6.1	1.1	head to waist
SLK 67-697		V24	—	1	5.2	2.8	1.0	"legs" & base
					3.9	3.9	—	base diameter
SLK 67-700	15:5	V24	—	1	6.0	5.6	1.0	neck to waist
SLK 67-701		V25	—	2	3.8	2.4	1.5	base
SLK 67-702		V25	—	2	4.5	2.6	1.3	"legs" & base
					3.7	3.2	—	base diameter
SLK 67-704	13:1	W42	2	5	12.0	5.5	—	neck to base
					3.2	2.7	—	base diameter
SLK 67-717		X43	2	2	7.4	2.6	1.3	fragment
SLK 67-834		W29	—	1	8.1	2.6	1.0	"legs" & base
					3.7	3.7	—	base diameter
SLK 67-844		—	—	0	4.8	4.0	2.4	"legs" & base
					5.4	3.8	—	base diameter
SLK 67-845		—	—	0	5.9	3.1	2.0	"legs" & base
					4.3	4.3	—	base diameter
SLK 67-846		—	—	0	4.1	2.0	1.0	"legs" & base
					2.7	2.7	—	base diameter
SLK 67-847		—	—	0	3.9	1.8	1.0	"legs" & base
					2.8	2.8	—	base diameter
SLK 67-848		—	—	0	8.6	2.6	1.3	base
SLK 67-849		—	—	0	6.0	2.1	—	"legs"
SLK 67-850		—	—	0	3.9	—	—	"legs" & base w/two rudimentary feet
						2.2	1.6	"legs"
						3.0	3.0	base
SLK 67-851		—	—	0	4.4	2.6	1.0	"legs" & base
					3.4	2.4	—	base diameter
SLK 67-852		—	—	0	4.6	2.4	1.0	"legs" & base
					3.1	2.8	—	base diameter
SLK 67-854		—	—	0	5.2	4.5	1.6	torso

REGISTRATION NUMBER	PLATE	SQUARE	AREA	LEVEL	HEIGHT	WIDTH	THICKNESS	DESCRIPTION
SLK 67-855		—	—	0	5.0	3.0	1.4	head & neck
SLK 67-856		—	—	0	5.0	3.3	1.8	head
SLK 67-857	16:10	—	—	0	4.9	3.8	1.1	head & shoulder fragment
SLK 67-858		—	—	0	4.2	2.0	1.4	head & neck
SLK 67-859	16:8	—	—	0	3.0	1.7	1.1	head
SLK 67-860	8:1	—	—	0	3.0	1.9	0.9	head
SLK 67-862		—	—	0	5.0	3.1	0.9	neck to waist
SLK 67-866		—	—	0	2.8	2.4	1.0	"legs" & base
					3.2	3.2	—	base diameter
SLK 67-871		—	—	0	4.0	2.9	1.3	neck to lower body
SLK 67-877				0	3.3	1.8	1.0	head
SLK 67-880	21:8	—	—	0	4.5	2.4	1.4	neck to base
SLK 67-882		W24	19	1	4.9	2.5	1.0	"legs" & base
					3.1	2.8	—	base diameter
SLK 67-885		—	—	0	3.6	3.5	0.8	torso
SLK 67-887		—	—	0	4.6	2.2	0.9	base
SLK 67-897	21:4	T25	—	1	5.4	3.5	2.7	"legs"
SLK 67-898		T25	—	1	4.9	2.0	1.5	base
SLK 67-899		T25	2	1	3.5	2.1	1.4	neck to waist
SLK 67-901		T25	1	1	2.7	2.1	1.4	"legs" & base
					3.0	3.0	—	base diameter
SLK 67-902		T25	—	1	4.4	2.6	1.1	base
SLK 67-903		T25	—	1	4.3	1.9	0.7	base
SLK 67-904	14:6	X25	16	1	6.1	3.5	1.1	neck to "legs"
SLK 67-910	5A:1	X25	15	1	15.8	6.2	—	complete except for head
					4.2	4.2	—	base diameter
SLK 67-911		X25	15	1	8.2	4.4	0.8	armpits to base
					3.7	3.7	—	base diameter
SLK 67-918		W24	1	1	6.5	2.7	1.1	frag. w/lower torso & "legs"
SLK 67-920		T25	2	1	4.4	2.5	1.1	"legs"
					4.4	4.4	—	base diameter
SLK 67-922		T25	2	1	3.4	2.2	0.9	base
					3.3	3.3	—	base diameter
SLK 67-924		T25	2	1	3.6	1.9	1.3	"legs" & base
					2.5	2.5	—	base diameter
SLK 67-925		U25		3	5.6	3.6	—	neck to base
SLK 67-926		V24	—	1	5.4	2.5	1.1	"legs" & base
					3.6	3.6	—	base diameter
SLK 67-927		V24	—	1	5.4	2.2	1.2	"legs" & base
					3.5	2.8	—	base diameter
SLK 67-930	7B:1	V24	—	1	7.3	5.8	—	bust w/arms missing
SLK 67-931		V24		1	4.4	2.4	1.6	"legs" & base
					3.6	3.6	—	base diameter
SLK 67-933		V24	—	1	3.7	2.0	1.0	head & neck
SLK 67-937		V24	—	1	4.8	2.5	1.6	"legs" & base
					3.6	3.6	—	base diameter

A. Terra-Cotta Human Figurines

REGISTRATION NUMBER	PLATE	SQUARE	AREA	LEVEL	HEIGHT	WIDTH	THICKNESS	DESCRIPTION
SLK 67-938	15:2	V24	—	1	7.8	5.7	1.1	neck to "legs"
SLK 67-939	3A:2	V24	—	1	3.1	2.6	3.2	head
SLK 67-941		V24	—	1	3.2	2.1	—	head
SLK 67-945	9:1	V24	—	3	11.3	7.0	1.9	head & torso
SLK 67-948		V24	—	2	6.9	2.2	0.9	base
SLK 67-952	7:3	V24	—	2	4.0	2.9	—	head
SLK 67-956		V24	—	1	9.0	2.9	1.3	"legs" & base
					3.4	2.8	—	base diameter
SLK 67-957		V24	—	1	3.8	3.7	0.8	torso
SLK 67-960	14:2	V24	—	3	5.9	3.4	1.0	torso
SLK 67-963		V24	—	3	5.0	3.5	1.7	head & neck
SLK 67-969		T25	2	1	6.1	3.0	1.2	base
SLK 67-971		T25	—	1	3.9	1.6	1.2	torso (rectangular in section) parts of 2 "legs"
SLK 67-974		T25	3	1	7.0	3.1	1.4	torso fragment
SLK 67-977		T25	3	1	6.4	2.9	1.3	base
SLK 67-978	14:3	T25	3	1	6.4	5.0	1.0	neck & torso
SLK 67-979		T25	3	1	5.7	3.9	2.0	"legs" & base
					6.0	6.0	—	base diameter
SLK 67-983		T25	2	1	3.9	2.6	1.3	base
SLK 67-984		T25	3	1	2.2	2.1	2.1	torso
SLK 67-986	16:7	T25	3	1	4.2	1.7	—	head
SLK 67-988		T25	3	1	5.6	1.8	0.9	base
SLK 67-990		T25	3	1	8.6	3.0	1.2	base
					3.2	2.9	—	base diameter
SLK 67-992		T25	3	1	8.5	2.1	1.6	base
					3.2	2.9	—	base diameter
SLK 67-993	13:4	T25	2	1	9.8	8.8	2.2	base of neck to waist
SLK 67-994	3A:3	S25	1	1	3.6	2.0	—	head
SLK 67-995		T25	3	2	6.0	5.0	0.8	torso
SLK 67-997		T25	3	1	3.0	1.8	1.0	fragment of necklace
SLK 67-998	3:3	T25	3	1	5.6	3.6	—	head
SLK 67-999		S24	1	1	3.0	2.8	1.4	"legs" & base
					3.5	3.1		base diameter
SLK 67-1000	6:3	S25	1	2	7.3	5.8	—	head to waist
SLK 67-1003		X25	18	2	4.5	2.0	1.2	base
					3.4	3.4	—	base diameter
SLK 67-1005	19:1	X25	16	2	4.6	2.2	—	head
SLK 67-1006		X25	16	1	7.5	3.1	1.7	base
SLK 67-1007		W24	1	1	3.6	2.3	1.2	"legs" fragment
SLK 67-1008		X25	16	2	8.0	5.0	1.3	neck to "legs"
SLK 67-1009		W24	1	1	4.7	4.4	1.0	shoulder to waist
SLK 67-1011	15:6	X25	16	2	5.9	5.0	1.8	neck to waist
SLK 67-1016		U25	NE quad	3	8.2	3.2	1.3	base
					4.1	3.4	—	base diameter
SLK 67-1017		Q26	1	4	5.0	2.8	1.9	legs
SLK 67-1020		S25	1	1	3.2	2.5	1.7	"legs" fragment

REGISTRATION NUMBER	PLATE	SQUARE	AREA	LEVEL	HEIGHT	WIDTH	THICKNESS	DESCRIPTION
SLK 67-1021		S25	2	3	2.5	2.4	—	base
SLK 67-1023		S25	2	2	6.3	6.2	2.0	upper torso fragment
SLK 67-1027		S25	1	3	8.5	6.2	—	head to waist
SLK 67-1032	17:2	S25	3	2	6.2	5.3	1.3	neck to waist
SLK 67-1040		S25	1	1	4.8	4.6	1.2	neck to waist
SLK 67-1041		S25	1	1	4.6	3.9	1.0	neck to waist
SLK 67-1045		S25	2	2	4.0	1.7	—	"legs" & base
					2.7	2.4	—	base diameter
SLK 67-1046		S25	1	2	3.8	2.3	1.2	base
SLK 67-1047		S25	2 south	2	5.0	2.6	1.0	"legs" & base
					2.8	2.8	—	base diameter
SLK 67-1052		Q26	14	2	3.2	2.3	1.1	base
SLK 67-1082	3:2	W24	—	5	4.0	2.5	—	head & neck
SLK 67-1083		W42	—	5	7.0	2.0	1.0	"legs" & base
					3.0	3.0	—	base diameter
SLK 67-1084	21:6	T25	3N	1	3.3	—	—	base
					1.4	1.4	—	leg diameter
					4.0	4.0	—	base diameter
SLK 67-1085	16:9	S25	1	3	3.5	2.0	—	head
SLK 67-1091		TVIII	2	2	5.2	3.9	1.2	torso
SLK 67-1092	15:7	TVIII	4	1	6.6	5.5	1.2	neck to waist
SLK 67-1113		S25	2	1	3.9	1.3	1.1	small, upper torso fragment
SLK 67-1115		S25	1	3	4.2	2.3	1.3	"legs" & base
					3.1	2.8	—	base dimensions
SLK 67-1117		T25	3	1	6.0	3.6	1.7	torso w/one arm stump
SLK 67-1119		S25	1	3	3.1	1.6	0.8	"legs" & base
					1.8	1.8	—	base diameter
SLK 67-1121		S25	2	1	5.3	4.3	1.0	base of neck to waist
SLK 67-1122		S25	1	3	6.4	3.1	—	neck to base
					2.3	2.1	—	base diameter
SLK 67-1123	13:2	S25	1	3	6.0	5.7	1.4	torso
SLK 67-1125	4:4	S25	2	3	5.9	5.1	1.7	neck to "legs"
SLK 67-1128	12:2	—	—	0	4.5	3.0	—	head & neck
SLK 67-1129		—	—	0	11.5	3.5	1.2	base
SLK 67-1130		—	—	0	3.1	2.0	1.1	"legs" & base
					2.9	2.7	—	base diameter
SLK 67-1131		—	—	0	4.7	3.2	1.1	frag. of legs
SLK 67-1132	20:1	—	—	0	3.3	2.7	1.3	head
SLK 67-1134		—	—	0	5.5	3.6	1.5	base of neck to breast
SLK 67-1156		S25	1	3	3.8	—	—	"legs" & base
					2.8	2.8	—	base diameter
					1.4	1.4	—	legs
SLK 67-1157		S25	6	2	4.6	2.0	1.7	base
SLK 67-1159		S25	4	2	5.7	1.8	1.3	"legs" & base
SLK 67-1161		S25	4	2	4.2	1.1	1.1	"legs" & base
					3.3	3.3	—	base diameter

A. Terra-Cotta Human Figurines

REGISTRATION NUMBER	PLATE	SQUARE	AREA	LEVEL	HEIGHT	WIDTH	THICKNESS	DESCRIPTION
SLK 67-1162		S25	1	3	4.5	2.1	1.1	"legs" & base
					3.1	2.7	–	base diameter
SLK 67-1163		S25	1	3	6.5	2.0	1.0	"legs" & base
					3.3	3.3	–	base diameter
SLK 67-1167		S25	1	3	5.6	3.9	1.0	upper torso fragment
SLK 67-1168		S25	1	3	5.0	4.7	1.0	torso
SLK 67-1169		S25	1	3	6.0	3.1	1.5	neck to "legs"
SLK 67-1170		S25	2	3	5.8	4.5	1.1	upper torso
SLK 67-1174	9:2	S25	1	3	5.2	2.8	–	head & neck
SLK 67-1178		S25	2	3	5.3	1.8	0.9	"legs" & base
					2.8	2.5	–	base diameter
SLK 67-1179		S25	5	2	3.8	1.4	–	"legs" & base
					2.6	2.6	–	base diameter
SLK 67-1181	8:2	S25	1	3	3.8	2.2	–	head
SLK 67-1182		S25	1	3	5.0	1.8	–	base
SLK 67-1183		W25	1	1	4.1	2.2	1.1	"legs" & base
					3.1	3.1	–	base diameter
SLK 67-1232		S25	2	2	6.3	2.8	1.4	base
SLK 67-1234		S25	1	3	4.8	3.2	1.0	torso
SLK 67-1235		T25	4	2	7.0	3.1	1.5	base
SLK 67-1240		S25	1	3	3.9	2.4	1.1	"legs" & base
					2.8	2.8	–	base diameter
SLK 67-1242		W25	–	1	8.2	3.3	2.1	base
SLK 67-1244		S25	7	2	5.6	2.9	1.2	"legs" & base
					4.1	4.1	–	base diameter
SLK 67-1245	11:3	U25	–	1	4.9	3.7	1.4	torso fragment
SLK 67-1246		W25	–	1	6.7	2.8	1.3	"legs" & base
					3.8	3.8	–	base diameter
SLK 67-1253	14:5	T VIII	1	1	3.2	2.7	0.9	torso
SLK 67-1268		–	–	0	7.8	2.3	1.0	leg fragment
SLK 67-1269		W25	NS balk	1	4.8	2.5	3.7	base
SLK 67-1272	4:3	–	–	0	5.7	5.1	1.3	shoulder to waist
SLK 67-1280		T VIII	2	2	5.8	2.4	1.5	"legs" & base
					4.1	4.1	–	base diameter
SLK 67-1281		T VIII	4	2	5.4	2.2	0.9	"legs" & base
SLK 67-1282		T VIII	3	1	4.6	2.8	1.3	"legs" & base
					4.0	4.0	–	base diameter
SLK 67-1285		W24	1	1	5.6	2.5	1.7	base
SLK 67-1286		W24	1	1	4.4	2.8	1.3	"legs" & base
					4.0	3.3	–	base diameter
SLK 67-1289		W24	1	1	3.0	2.5	1.3	"legs" & base
					4.4	4.4	–	base diameter
SLK 67-1291	21:3	V43		dump	4.4	1.6	–	head & torso
SLK 67-1292		V43		dump	5.6	2.3	1.8	"legs" & base
					2.8	2.4	–	base diameter
SLK 67-1322		V24		1	4.4	4.0	1.2	shoulder to waist
SLK 67-1323		U25		2	4.1	1.2	–	"legs" & base
					2.4	2.4	–	base diameter

REGISTRATION NUMBER	PLATE	SQUARE	AREA	LEVEL	HEIGHT	WIDTH	THICKNESS	DESCRIPTION
SLK 67-1324		—	—	0	4.5	3.1	1.0	torso
SLK 67-1481		S25	2	1	3.1	2.0	1.2	"legs" & base
					3.7	3.7	—	base diameter
SLK 67-1482		S25	6	2	4.2	2.8	1.2	legs
SLK 67-1484		S251	7	2	5.5	3.7	1.8	"legs" & base
					4.2	2.2	—	base dimensions
SLK 67-1492		X25	—	2	4.5	2.3	1.0	legs
SLK 67-1493		X25	—	1	2.6	2.3	1.5	"legs" & base
					3.8	3.8	—	base diameter
SLK 67-1494		X25	—	2	3.6	1.7	0.7	"legs" & base
					3.0	3.0	—	base diameter
SLK 67-1495		X25	—	1	5.0	4.9	1.2	torso
SLK 67-1496		Y24	—	2	4.9	3.2	2.0	"legs" & base
					4.4	2.9	—	base diameter
SLK 67-1498		—	—	0	4.2	3.2	1.0	torso
SLK 67-1497		—	—	0	2.7	—	—	"legs" & base
						3.3	—	base diameter
SLK 67-1499		—	—	0	5.8	—	—	"legs" & base
					4.0	3.0	—	base dimensions
SLK 67-1500		—	—	0	3.5	2.5	1.0	head
SLK 67-1501		—	—	0	4.7	2.6	1.0	"legs" & base
SLK 67-1503		—	—	0	5.8	4.1	1.2	fragment
SLK 67-1504		—	—	0	3.5	2.9	1.2	fragment
SLK 67-1506		—	—	0	3.4	2.4	—	head
SLK 67-1507		—	—	0	5.5	3.2	1.3	"legs" & base
					4.8	4.2	—	base diameter
SLK 67-1508		—	—	0	4.6	2.5	1.3	"legs" & base
					3.2	3.0		base diameter
SLK 67-1509		—	—	0	4.9	3.8	1.4	base of neck to waist
SLK 67-1511		—	—	0	4.6	1.7	—	head
SLK 67-1513		—	—	0	4.4	3.0	0.9	torso
SLK 67-1514		—	—	0	3.4	2.7	—	head
SLK 67-1515		—	—	0	3.5	1.9	—	head & neck
SLK 67-1516		—	—	0	3.2	2.1	—	head
SLK 67-1517		—	—	0	4.2	2.4	0.7	torso
SLK 67-1518		—	—	0	2.6	1.8	—	head
SLK 67-1519		—	—	0	4.8	2.3	1.6	"legs" & base
					3.0	2.5	—	base diameter
SLK 67-1520		—	—	0	2.7	2.4	—	"legs" & base
					4.0	4.0	—	base diameter
SLK 67-1527		—	—	0	4.0	2.4	1.3	head
SLK 67-1528		—	—	0	3.3	2.1	—	head
SLK 67-1529		—	—	0	4.0	2.9	1.0	torso
SLK 67-1530	20:2	—	—	0	2.9	2.0	1.0	head & neck
SLK 67-1531		—	—	0	4.0	3.9	0.9	torso
SLK 67-1535		—	—	0	4.8	4.1	0.7	torso
SLK 67-1536		—	—	0	7.2	3.3	1.2	torso
SLK 67-1537		—	—	0	6.0	2.4	1.2	"legs" & base
					4.3	3.8	—	base diameter

A. Terra-Cotta Human Figurines

REGISTRATION NUMBER	PLATE	SQUARE	AREA	LEVEL	HEIGHT	WIDTH	THICKNESS	DESCRIPTION
SLK 67-1538		—	—	0	5.8	4.0	1.2	torso
SLK 67-1539		—	—	0	8.0	5.1	4.2	torso
SLK 67-1540		—	—	0	5.4	3.7	1.5	neck
SLK 67-1545		—	—	0	6.1	2.6	1.1	base
SLK 67-1542		—	—	0	3.8	2.0	0.8	leg fragment
SLK 67-1551		X24	1	1	6.4	3.2	—	"legs" & base
					2.9	2.4	—	base diameter
SLK 67-1553		Y24	1	1	7.3	3.0	1.5	legs
SLK 67-1556		X24	—	1	2.5	2.2	0.7	base
SLK 67-1565		—	—	0	2.9	2.7	1.9	head
WRD 67-1	12:4	—	—	0	11.4	9.4	2.4	neck to waist
WRD 67-2	15:1	—	—	0	4.8	4.5	1.1	neck to waist
WRD 67-31	17:3	TR3	—	1	8.0	7.4	1.9	neck to waist
WRD 67-36		TR3	2	2	4.5	1.2	—	"legs" & base
					3.6	3.1	—	base diameter
WRD 67-43		—	—	0	5.0	4.3	1.0	neck & torso
WRD 67-509		—	—	0	15.8	5.5	2.9	head
WRD 67-564		Tomb N	—	—	2.7	2.1	1.0	base

CATALOGUE B

TERRA-COTTA ANIMAL FIGURINES

REGISTRATION NUMBER SLK-*	PLATE	SQUARE	AREA	LEVEL	HEIGHT	WIDTH	THICKNESS	DESCRIPTION
S. Surf. 153	–	–	–	0	5.5	3.4	2.5	headless quadruped
S. Surf. 154	–	–	–	0	7.2	6.7	5.6	foreparts of headless quadruped
S. Surf. 155	–	–	–	0	5.5	3.2	2.7	foreparts of quadruped
SI 1 2	–	–	–	1	4.5	3.7	2.3	quadruped torso
SI 1B 24	25:1	–	6	1B	9.7	2.3	2.3	bull head with crescent-shaped horns
SI 1B 28	–	–	4	1B	4.3	3.9	2.0	
SI 1B 29	–	–	4	1B	4.8	4.2	2.2	
SI 1B 44	–	–	7	1B	7.2	7.0		horn
SI 1B 52	25:2	–	1	1B	7.5	3.3	3.0	bull head with crescent-shaped horns
SI 1B 99	–	–	2	1B				
SI 1B 102	–	–	2	1B	3.0	2.8	1.8	head
SI 2 66	–	–	1	2	7.8	4.5	3.6	
SI 2 75	23:2	–	3	2	4.0	3.5	1.4	horse, head & neck
SI 2 77	23:1	–	3	2	3.9	2.8	1.5	horse, head & neck
SI 2 82	–	–	3	2	4.0	2.8	–	
SI 2 102	25:3	–	–	–	–	–	–	bull
67-14	–	–	–	0	4.5	1.3	2.6	pedestal of bird on pedestal
67-15	29:2	–	–	0	4.3	2.5	1.5	bird on pedestal base, base & tail only
67-22	–	–	–	0	4.5	4.2	1.7	headless forequarter of quadruped
67-27	–	–	–	0	4.5	2.6	2.1	legless hindquarters of quadruped

*Except where preceded by another prefix.

B. Terra-Cotta Animal Figurines

REGISTRATION NUMBER SLK-	PLATE	SQUARE	AREA	LEVEL	HEIGHT	WIDTH	THICKNESS	DESCRIPTION
67-28	–	–	–	0	6.5	4.0	2.0	headless quadruped
67-36	–	–	–	0	3.6	2.8	1.5	equid (?) head
67-46	–	–	–	0	6.2	2.8	1.8	
67-52	–	Q27	8	1	6.3	6.0	4.8	foreparts of crescent-horned bull
67-62	–	Q27	2	2	4.0	3.0	2.7	torso fragment
67-64	–	Q27	1	2	5.0	4.6	3.7	foreparts of headless quadruped
67-68	28:1	Q27	12	1	4.1	3.7	1.1	headless bird on pedestal base
67-69	–	Q27	12	1	4.8	2.5	2.0	torso of quadruped
67-85	–	–	–	0	4.5	2.3	2.2	torso of quadruped
67-152	25:5	–	–	0	3.0	2.1		head of bull (?)
67-166	–	Q26	7	1	4.1	2.8	1.9	headless quadruped
67-191	–	–	–	0	5.0	2.4	1.3	headless quadruped
67-209	–	R26	4	1	2.8	2.6	1.5	headless quadruped
67-210	–	–	3	1	5.5	2.8	2.3	headless quadruped
67-216	25:7	R26	4	1	4.0	3.4	1.1	head of bull (?) with long muzzle
67-227	25:6	Q26	6	2	5.2	3.7	2.0	head of bull
67-233	–	Q26	7	2	4.2	2.8	2.2	bull (?) complete
67-234	–	Q26	7	2	5.2	4.5	3.2	head and foreparts of bull (?)
67-256	27:2	Q26	7	2	8.0	5.5	3.0	sheep
67-260	–	Q26	7	2	3.4	2.5	1.3	headless quadruped
67-289	–	W43	3	4	7.8	6.0	3.1	horned bull
67-295	24:2	R26	–	1	5.2	3.8	1.7	horse ?
67-296	–	R26	4	1	5.0	2.8	2.5	headless quadruped
67-301	–	–	–	0	3.2	2.5	1.2	head of horse (?)
67-304	–	–	–	0	3.4	2.5	1.6	torso fragment of quadruped
67-305	–	–	–	0	5.0	3.9	2.5	torso of quadruped
67-306	–	–	–	0	6.0	3.1	2.5	torso fragment of quadruped
67-307	–	–	–	0	4.8	3.7	2.4	torso of quadruped

REGISTRATION NUMBER SLK-	PLATE	SQUARE	AREA	LEVEL	HEIGHT	WIDTH	THICKNESS	DESCRIPTION
67-308	–	–	–	0	4.8	3.5	2.8	horse head
67-309	–	–	–	0	5.2	2.7	2.6	torso of quadruped
67-341	–	Q26	14	2	3.0	2.4	1.6	torso fragment of quadruped
67-343	–	Q26	6	1	4.3	2.3	2.0	forepart of quadruped
67-344	–	Q26	6	1	2.0	1.2	1.2	horn of bull
67-346	–	Q26	6	1	4.5	2.7	1.8	torso fragment of quadruped
67-352	26:4	R26	4	1	6.2	5.0	1.3	bull (?)
67-356	–	Q26	2	1	6.0	2.6	2.4	head fragment
67-372	–	V43		4	6.9	4.2	3.5	torso of quadruped
67-374	26:4	V43	–	5	5.5	5.4	1.9	bull
67-379	–	V43	–	6	5.3	3.9	3.0	torso & two legs of quadruped
67-380	–	V43	–	4	5.1	3.1	3.1	head, neck & traces of forelegs of bull (?)
67-397	–	Y25	A7	1	7.2	4.0	3.5	torso of quadruped
67-402	–	near Y25	–	0	3.6	2.2	2.1	torso, traces of legs of quadruped
67-409	–	R26	4	2	3.4	2.1	1.8	hindquarters of quadruped
67-410	–	V43	–	7	4.4	3.5	2.5	legless quadruped
67-411	–	V43	–	7	5.2	4.3	2.2	legless quadruped
67-414	–	V43	–	7	4.0	3.6	3.3	hindquarters of quadruped
67-427	26:1	Y25	B2	1	4.9	3.6	3.2	head & neck of bull (?)
67-440	–	Y25	G7	1	4.3	2.2	1.3	torso & two legs of quadruped
67-444	–	V25	–	1	3.4	3.0	2.8	rump & tail of quadruped
67-460	29:3	V25	–	1	5.6	5.1	2.5	headless bird on pedestal base
67-469	–	R26	2	1	4.0	3.2	2.1	head to upper part of forequarters of quadruped
67-500	–	–	–	0	4.8	2.3	1.5	goat (?)
67-501	–	–	–	0	3.2	1.5	1.4	head of quadruped

B. Terra-Cotta Animal Figurines

REGISTRATION NUMBER SLK-	PLATE	SQUARE	AREA	LEVEL	HEIGHT	WIDTH	THICKNESS	DESCRIPTION
67-503	25:4	—	—	0	5.6	5.4	2.1	bull head
67-504	—	—	—	0	6.5	3.8	2.8	torso & one leg of quadruped
67-505	—	—	—	0	4.4	2.1	1.6	head fragment & long neck of quadruped
67-506	—	—	—	0	6.0	3.5	3.5	torso & one leg of quadruped
67-507	—	—	—	0	4.9	3.6	3.0	torso & parts of neck & legs of quadruped
67-508	—	—	—	0	4.2	2.1	1.9	torso & parts of legs of quadruped
67-509	—	—	—	0	5.2	3.0	2.7	hindquarters of quadruped
67-511	—	—	—	0	5.1	2.4	2.1	torso fragment of quadruped
67-513	—	—	—	0	3.9	2.6	2.2	torso fragment & one hind leg of quadruped
67-514	—	—	—	0	3.1	2.5	2.0	rump of quadruped
67-522	—	X25	2F9	1	4.6	2.0	2.0	head & long neck of quadruped
67-524	—	X25	2F8	1	3.2	3.1	1.8	head & neck of horse
67-529	—	W25	H9	1	4.7	2.7	1.7	head & neck of horse
67-542	27:1	V25	—	1	5.6	4.5	2.6	head & legs missing—donkey (?)
67-563	—	V25	—	1	4.7	2.1	1.7	torso of quadruped
67-586	—	W25	4	1	4.1	3.5	2.0	hindquarters of quadruped
67-619	—	V25	—	2	4.3	2.6		quadruped, legs missing
67-628	—	W25	1	1	7.0	3.9	3.0	headless quadruped
67-641	—	W25	2	1	5.9	3.1	3.0	headless quadruped
67-642	24:4	W24	1	1	4.5	2.3	1.3	horse with blinders (?)
67-649	—	W24	1	1	3.5	2.8	2.6	head with stubby horns
67-661	—	V25	—	2	7.1	2.9	2.9	torso of quadruped
67-663	—	V25	—	2	4.2	2.0	2.0	torso of quadruped

REGISTRATION NUMBER SLK-	PLATE	SQUARE	AREA	LEVEL	HEIGHT	WIDTH	THICKNESS	DESCRIPTION
67-664	–	V25	–	2	6.5	4.0	3.4	torso of quadruped
67-668	29:1	V24	–	2	6.6	4.6		bird on pedestal base, head missing
67-671	–	V24	–	1	5.8	3.1	3.0	torso of quadruped
67-672	–	V24	–	1	3.7	3.2	2.7	neck & upper torso fragment of quadruped
67-678	–	V24	–	1	8.1	6.1	3.0	torso & one leg of quadruped
67-682	–	V24	–	1	3.7	2.5	2.2	torso & hind legs of quadruped
67-688	–	Y24	1	1	3.0	2.5	2.0	torso & hind legs of quadruped
67-696	–	V25	–	2	9.2	5.0	4.2	torso of quadruped
67-698	30:1	V24	–	2	7.4	5.5	2.6	headless bird on narrow pedestal base
67-699	28:2	V24	–	2	5.5	5.4		bird on narrow pedestal base
67-831	–	Y25	10	2	5.1	2.4	1.7	torso of quadruped
67-833	–	X25	3	1	6.8	2.9	2.9	torso of quadruped
67-853	–	–	–	0	5.3	4.2	3.6	hindquarters of quadruped
67-861	–	–	–	0	4.5	2.2	1.7	torso, parts of legs of quadruped
67-869	–	–	–	0	5.5	3.4	2.8	torso & parts of legs of quadruped
67-872	–	–	–	0	3.2	2.1	1.7	hindquarters, parts of legs
67-874	–	–	–	0	5.3	2.6	2.6	torso, parts of extremities of quadruped
67-876	–	–	–	0	5.0	2.7	2.3	torso & parts of extremities of quadruped
67-896	–	T25	1	1	5.2	3.1	2.4	foreparts of quadruped
67-905	–	W25	4	1	4.7	3.2	2.2	foreparts of equid figurine
67-906	–	W25	4	1	4.8	2.3	2.2	torso & parts of extremities of quadruped

B. Terra-Cotta Animal Figurines

REGISTRATION NUMBER SLK-	PLATE	SQUARE	AREA	LEVEL	HEIGHT	WIDTH	THICKNESS	DESCRIPTION
67-916	–	V24	–	3	7.4	5.3	3.0	equid figure, legs missing
67-929	–	V24	–	1	4.9	2.9	2.2	torso & parts of extremities of quadruped
67-935	–	V24	–	1	3.2	2.8	2.7	foreparts of headless quadruped
67-936	24:1	V24	–	1	5.5	3.0	1.8	equid head & neck
67-940	–	V24	–	1	3.4	2.5	2.0	parts of forepart of headless quadruped
67-949	–	V24	–	3	6.0	5.0	3.6	torso & parts of extremities of headless quadruped
67-958	23:3	V24	–	1	4.9	2.1	2.0	horse
67-962	–	V24	–	3	8.2	4.5	2.5	torso & one leg of quadruped
67-972	–	T25	North	1	4.3			bird
67-976	28:3	T25	2	1	4.4	3.6	2.5	bird on pedestal, head & part of tail missing
67-982	–	T25	2	1	4.2	1.5		bird
67-985	–	T25	3	1	4.8	2.1		torso fragment of quadruped
67-1022	–	S25	2	3	3.2	3.1	2.8	head
67-1031	–	S25	3	2	2.9	2.8	1.3	rump & one hind leg of quadruped
67-1049	–	S25	1	2	4.0	2.0	1.8	torso fragment of quadruped
67-1088	–	TVIII	1	1	7.3	2.7	2.3	torso & parts of extremities of quadruped
67-1109	24:5	S25	3	1	3.2	1.6	1.2	horse's (?) head
67-1110	–	S25	1	3	3.2	3.0	2.0	bird on pedestal base
67-1114	–	?	7	3	2.8	2.5	2.5	rump of quadruped
67-1118	–	T25	3	1	2.4	1.9		mutilated animal head, horns missing
67-1133	–	–	–	0	5.9	3.1	2.8	torso of quadruped
67-1166	23:4	S25	1	2	3.5	3.3	1.8	equid (?) head
67-1180	–	S25	1	3	2.6	1.8		headless bird on pedestal base
67-1189	–	W24	–	2	4.4	1.6		animal (?) head

REGISTRATION NUMBER SLK-	PLATE	SQUARE	AREA	LEVEL	HEIGHT	WIDTH	THICKNESS	DESCRIPTION
67-1236	–	S25	1	3	2.5	1.4		fragmentary head
67-1237	–	T25	4	2	4.7	2.9	2.3	torso of quadruped
67-1239	–	S25	1	3	2.8	2.2	2.0	torso & parts of foreparts' extremities
67-1252	–	TVIII	1	1	4.1	3.4		horned head
67-1262	–	–	–	0	3.4	2.5	2.0	head w/horns missing
67-1270	–	W25	N-S balk	1	4.1	3.5	3.3	rump & part of hind legs
67-1287	–	W24	1	2	4.5	2.8	2.7	torso & parts of extremities of quadruped
67-1288	–	W24	1	2	5.0	4.5	3.2	hindquarters of quadruped, one leg missing
67-1290	–	V43	–	dump	8.1	4.5	4.5	torso of bovid
67-1500	–	–	–	0	4.6	3.2		foreparts of headless bovid
67-1505	–	–	–	0	9.8	1.8		hindquarters of bovid
67-1510	–	–	–	0	3.8	2.0		foreparts of headless bovid
67-1512	–	–	–	0	5.4	4.3	2.6	bird (?)
67-1525	–	–	–	0	3.4	2.2	1.9	torso of bovid
67-1543	–	–	–	0	3.6	2.7	1.8	torso of bovid
67-1544	–	–	–	0	3.5	3.2		bull
67-1545	–	–	–	0	4.5	2.8	2.0	torso of bovid
WRD 67-30	–	TR1	1	2	5.3	3.5	3.4	animal body
WRD 67-33	–	TR2	–	1	3.8	3.1	1.7	dog (?)
WRD 67-41	–	TR4	–	1	3.8	2.6	1.9	animal hindquarters
WRD 67-44	26:3	–	–	0	4.6	3.9	2.3	bull (?)
WRD 67-45	24:3	–	–	0	4.5	2.1	1.8	head & neck of horse (?)
WRD 67-91	–	–	–	0	7.5	4.7	3.0	torso, head w/mane
WRD 67-92	–	–	–	0	4.1	3.1	2.4	torso & leg fragment w/punctuate dots
WRD 67-291	–	Tomb 3	–	–	7.5	4.9	2.6	bull
WRD 67-297	–	Tomb 3	–	–	3.8	3.1	1.2	animal horns
WRD 67-304	–	Tomb 3	–	–	5.8	3.4	3.2	torso & parts of extremities of bovid

CATALOGUE C

ANIMAL AND RIDER FIGURINES

REGISTRATION NUMBER	PLATE	SQUARE	AREA	LEVEL	HEIGHT	WIDTH	THICKNESS	DESCRIPTION
SI 1B 57			2	1B	6.2	5.2	2.2	rider missing
SLK 67-164				0	6.4	4.0	3.2	back of animal chipped
SLK 67-206	30:3	R26	3	1	6.3	4.8	2.6	only traces of side saddle of rider remain
SLK 67-443		V25		1	5.8	2.1	1.6	back of animal chipped
SLK 67-475				0	5.0	2.8	2.5	back of horse chipped; rider (?) missing
SLK 67-510				0	4.5	3.6	3.0	neck & torso of animal, top of back broken, rider (?) missing
SLK 67-512				0	6.0	3.2	2.8	neck & torso of riderless figurine, top of back missing, two lumps of clay applied to sides
SLK 67-592	28:4	W25	3	1	7.4	4.6	2.1	equid figurine with rider on back
SLK 67-622		V25		2	6.3	3.8	3.3	animal w/pinched mane; side saddle rider (?) broken off back
SLK 67-683	28:5	V24		1	5.4	5.3	3.1	fragment of rider on back of animal
SLK 67-685	28:6	V24		1	5.8	3.9	2.7	headless animal w/parts of legs of rider
SLK 67-878				0	5.1	3.7	2.1	body of animal w/parts of leg of rider

REGISTRATION NUMBER	PLATE	SQUARE	AREA	LEVEL	HEIGHT	WIDTH	THICKNESS	DESCRIPTION
SLK 67-886				0	5.0	3.8	2.2	torso of animal, rider broken away
SLK 67-895	30:2	W24	19	1	6.6	5.1	2.1	equid figurine w/headless rider
SLK 67-900		T25	1	1	3.1	2.2	1.6	animal torso w/one leg, rider missing
SLK 67-921		V24		3	4.6	3.2	2.3	animal w/fragment of rider
SLK 67-928		V24		1	4.7	3.4	2.4	back of animal chipped, carried rider (?)
SLK 67-934		V24		1	5.1	2.4		torso & tail of animal & neck, torso & legs of rider
SLK 67-943		V24		2	4.5	2.1	1.3	rider missing
SLK 67-955	28:7	V24		1	5.0	3.4	2.8	animal w/mane, part of rider
SLK 67-1001		V24		3	5.4	3.9	3.8	one flank of animal has 2 tips & clay strips of rider (?), yet back almost smooth
SLK 67-1025		S25	4	2	5.6	2.5	2.3	rider missing
SLK 67-1126		S25	2	3	4.0	3.3	2.1	back chipped, rider missing
SLK 67-1160		S25	1	2	5.2	3.3	2.5	rider missing
SLK 67-1164	30A:1	S25	1	3	4.5	4.0		upper part of rider figure (?)
SLK 67-1165		S25	1	3	3.0	2.6	2.0	upper part of animal torso
SLK 67-1273				0	5.0	3.3	2.2	back of animal chipped
SLK 67-1524				0	3.7	2.4	1.8	torso, tail & hindquarters of animal w/ traces of legs of rider
SLK 67-1552		Y24	1	1	4.3	4.0	2.2	animal figurine w/mane, rider (?) missing

CATALOGUE D

CHARIOTS AND WAGONS

REGISTRATION NUMBER SLK-*	PLATE	SQUARE	AREA	LEVEL	HEIGHT	WIDTH	THICKNESS	DESCRIPTION
S. Surf. 152		—	—	0	8.8	3.0		chariot body
S. Surf. 156		—	—	0	3.9	3.9	1.7	wheel
S. Surf. 157		—	—	0	4.4	4.4	1.7	wheel
SI 1 32		—	—	1	6.2	4.8	3.3	chariot body
SI 1 81		—	3	1	4.5	4.5	1.4	wheel
SI 1B 59		—	4	1B	4.2	4.2	1.0	wheel
SI 1B 90		—	—	1B	5.5	5.5	2.2	wheel
SI 1B 101		—	3	1B	6.1	6.1	2.8	wheel
SI 1B 145		—	1	1B	3.7	0.8		wheel
SI 1B 146		—	1	1B	4.2	1.2		chariot body
SI 2 34		—	1	2	5.5	5.5	1.3	wheel
SI 2 35		—	1	2	3.5	3.5	1.6	wheel
SI 2 69		—	3	2	4.2	4.2	2.1	wheel
67-24		—	—	0	3.6	2.0		wheel
					2.2	2.2		wheel
67-25		—	—	0	3.5	3.3	2.2	wheel
67-26		—	—	0	4.2	4.1	1.3	fragment
67-33	33:3	—	—	0	5.0	4.5	1.5	fragment
67-35	33:1	—	—	0	5.5	4.6	1.2	chariot
67-43		Q27	6	1	4.1	3.2	1.0	model bed fragment
67-44		—	—	0	4.8	3.8	2.2	wheel
67-51		W41	—	bs	5.6	5.6	1.2	wheel
67-61		Q27	2	2	6.2	6.2	1.3	wheel
67-80		W43	1	3	5.1	5.1	1.1	wheel
67-87		—	—	0	4.1	4.1	1.9	chariot fragment
67-88		—	—	0	5.3	5.3	1.1	wheel
67-89		—	—	0	6.6	6.6	1.8	wheel
67-135		Q27	2	2	6.8	6.8	1.1	wheel
67-145	32:4	—	—	0	8.1	5.0	1.8	chariot or wagon fragment
67-159		—	—	0	3.8	3.5	1.6	wheel
67-160		—	—	0	2.6	2.4	1.0	chariot fragment
67-177		—	—	0	4.2	3.2	0.9	wheel
67-178		—	—	0	4.4	4.4	1.3	wheel
67-286		Q26	1	1	2.9	2.3	0.6	fragment
67-302		—	—	0	6.8	5.2	5.0	fragment
67-322		—	—	0	4.0	3.1		fragment
67-338		Q26	14	2	5.2	5.2	2.6	wheel
67-351		R26	3	1	1.9	0.6		wheel
					5.8	5.8		wheel diameter

*Except where preceded by another prefix.

REGISTRATION NUMBER SLK-	PLATE	SQUARE	AREA	LEVEL	HEIGHT	WIDTH	THICKNESS	DESCRIPTION
67-354	33:2	R26	4	1	5.2	6.4	1.0	chariot
67-364		X43	2	3	3.9	3.9		diameter
					1.5	0.8		wheel
67-376		V43	–	6	3.0	1.2		wheel
					6.2	6.2		wheel diameter
67-395		Q26	11	2	7.5	5.5	0.8	chariot fragment
67-406		R26	1	2	7.0	7.0	2.0	wheel
67-413		V43	–	7	1.2	0.3	0.3	wheel
67-420		Y25	H7	1	8.0	8.0	2.8	wheel
67-424		R26	3	1	5.7	4.1	1.0	chariot fragment
67-439		Y25	E2	1	4.7	4.7	2.0	wheel
67-495		–	–	0	6.7	6.3	3.2	chariot fragment
67-496		–	–	0	6.4	6.4	3.8	wheel
67-497		–	–	0	4.2	4.2	2.3	wheel
67-498		–	–	0	5.6	5.6	2.2	wheel
67-530		X25	2	1	7.9	2.5		wheel
					9.0	9.0		diameter
67-535		Y25	3	1	5.1	5.1	1.1	wheel
67-544		V25	–	1	4.2	3.8	1.0	chariot fragment
67-546	32:2	V25	–	1	5.7	5.1	3.5	necklace fragment
67-573		W25	1	1	5.0	5.0	2.2	wheel
67-593		W25	3	1	4.8	4.8	1.4	wheel
67-627		W25	3	1	3.9	3.9	2.0	wheel
67-630		W25	1	1	5.9	5.9	2.5	wheel
67-648		W24	1	1	4.1	4.1	1.3	wheel
67-667		V24	–	3	6.8	6.8	3.2	wheel
67-669	31:3	V24	–	2	6.6	4.0	3.2	fragment
67-675		V24	–	1	5.6	5.6	2.8	wheel
67-693		W28	2	1	4.4	4.4	3.0	wheel
67-703		V24	–	1	6.2	6.2	2.2	wheel
67-832		W25	–	1	5.5	5.5	2.2	wheel
67-707		V24	–	1	4.2	4.2	2.1	wheel
67-836		W25	–	1	6.1	5.5	5.0	chariot
67-863		–	–	0	6.8	6.8	2.7	wheel
67-864		–	–	0	3.9	3.9	1.7	wheel
67-865		–	–	0	5.4	5.4	2.8	wheel
67-867		–	–	0	10.0	6.6	4.9	chariot fragment
67-873	32:3	–	–	0	5.5	4.7	4.6	wagon fragment
67-879		–	–	0	4.3	4.3	2.1	wheel
67-894	32:1	X25	Wall M	1	12.8	8.1	4.0	chariot fragment
67-893		–	–	0	7.4	4.0	2.7	chariot fragment
67-923		X25	16	2	5.8	5.8	2.7	wheel
67-932		V24	–	1	4.6	4.6	2.6	wheel
67-947		V24	–	3	6.4	6.4	2.8	wheel
67-950		V24	–	1	4.9	4.9	1.3	wheel
67-951		V24	–	3	6.8	6.8	1.8	wheel
67-953	31:4	V24	–	2	6.5	4.5	3.0	chariot (?)

D. Chariots and Wagons

REGISTRATION NUMBER SLK-	PLATE	SQUARE	AREA	LEVEL	HEIGHT	WIDTH	THICKNESS	DESCRIPTION
67-954		V24	—	3	11.6	9.3	3.9	chariot fragment
67-980	31:1	T25	2	1	6.6	5.0	3.6	wagon
67-981		T25	3	1	3.9	3.9	2.3	wheel
67-989		T25	1	1	8.2	8.2	4.4	wheel
67-1018		U25	—	3	6.7	6.7	3.6	wheel
67-1029		S25	3	2	7.0	7.0	1.1	wheel
67-1033		R26	1	2	5.0	5.0	2.3	wheel
67-1043		S25	1	2	5.0	5.0	2.0	wheel
67-1081		S1	—	0	5.5	5.5	1.8	wheel
67-1116		Y25	B8	2	3.9	3.9	1.0	wheel
67-1120		S25	3	3	6.1	6.1	2.9	wheel
67-1158		T25	3	1	4.3	4.2	3.6	fragment
67-1177		S25	1	2	9.9	4.6		fragment
67-1233		U25		2	6.9	6.9	3.0	wheel
67-1247		S25	1	3	4.6	4.6	2.7	wheel
67-1248	31:2	T25	4	2	6.9	5.2	3.1	fragment
67-1325		Y25	—	2	6.6	6.6	1.3	wheel
67-1488		S25	1	2	4.2	3.5		chariot fragment
67-1521		—	—	0	4.2	4.2	4.2	wheel
67-1523		—	—	0	4.8	4.8	2.2	wheel
67-1526		—	—	0	2.1	2.1	2.0	wheel
WRD 67-3	34:1	—	—	0	7.3	4.8	1.2	wagon
WRD 67-28		TR1	2	2	3.2	0.9		wheel
					8.0	8.0		wheel diameter
WRD 67-94		—	—	0	6.3	6.3	1.7	wheel
WRD 67-95		—	—	0	2.3	1.0		wheel
					5.5	5.5		wheel diameter
WRD 67-396		—	—	0	5.0	4.0	1.8	chariot fragment

PLATE 1

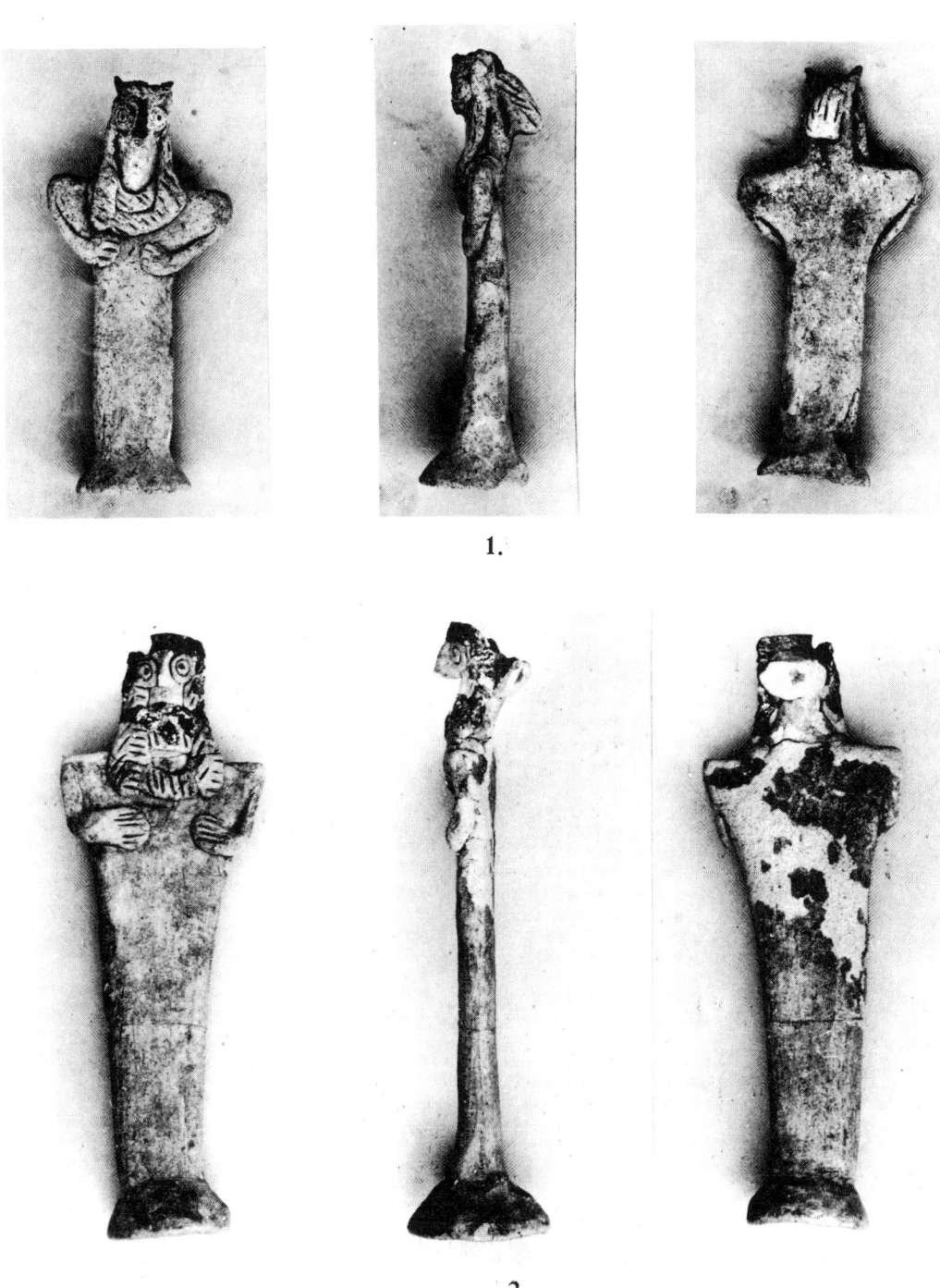

PLATE 1
Catalogue A

1. SLK 67-526, Type IA. Complete, with circular concave base. Buff pottery, burned (?), grey at top.

2. SLK 67-684, Type IA. Bitumen applied to hair coils and the choker necklace.

PLATE 2

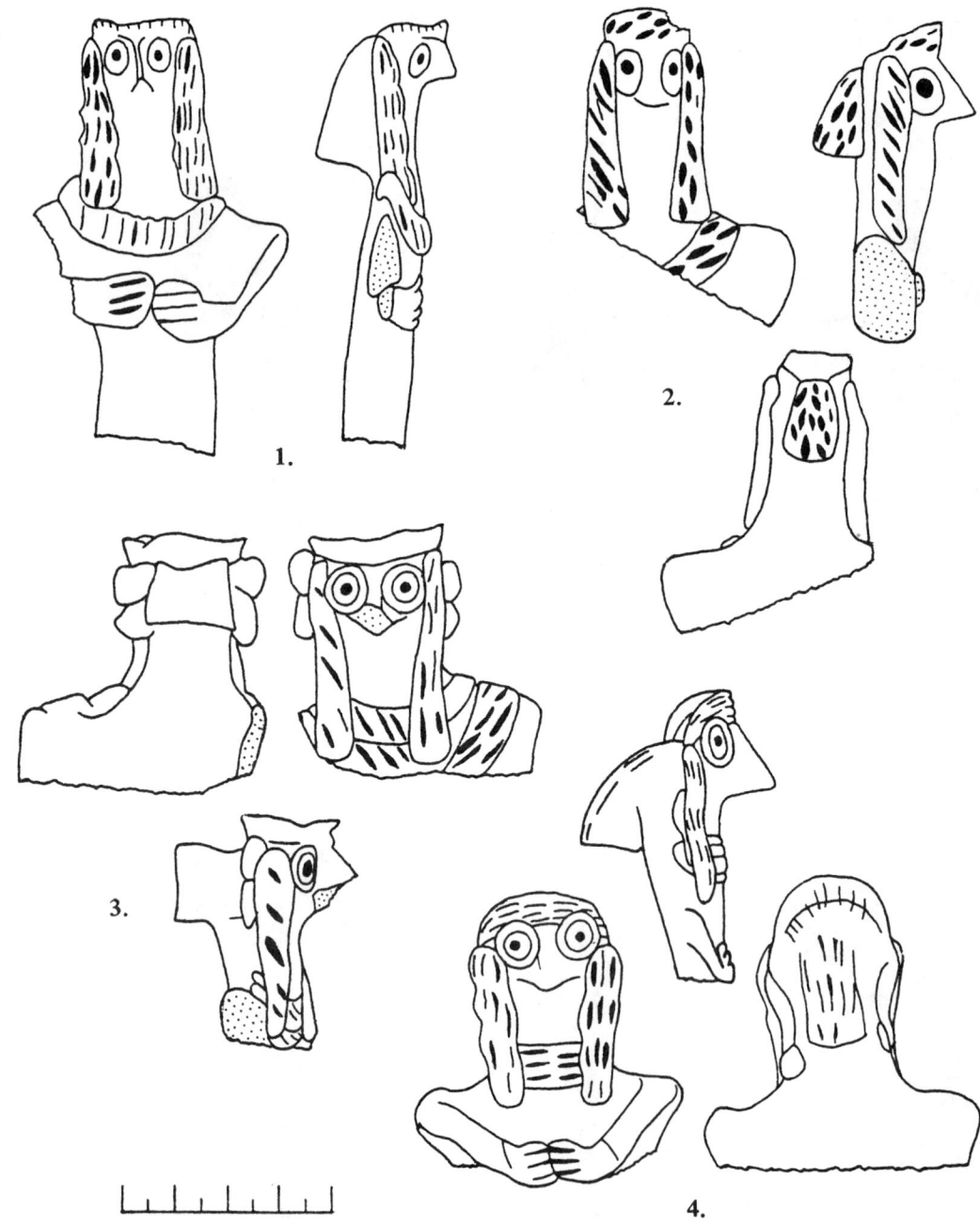

PLATE 2
Catalogue A

1. SLK 67-476, Type IA. Pinched pony tail with no decoration. Marking around outer edges of applied eye pellets.

2. SLK 67-125, Type IA. Head, left shoulder.

3. SLK 67-1, Type IA. Bust of female figurine, with prominent rectangular bun behind.

4. SLK 67-42, Type IA. Female figurine with pony tail, choker necklace.

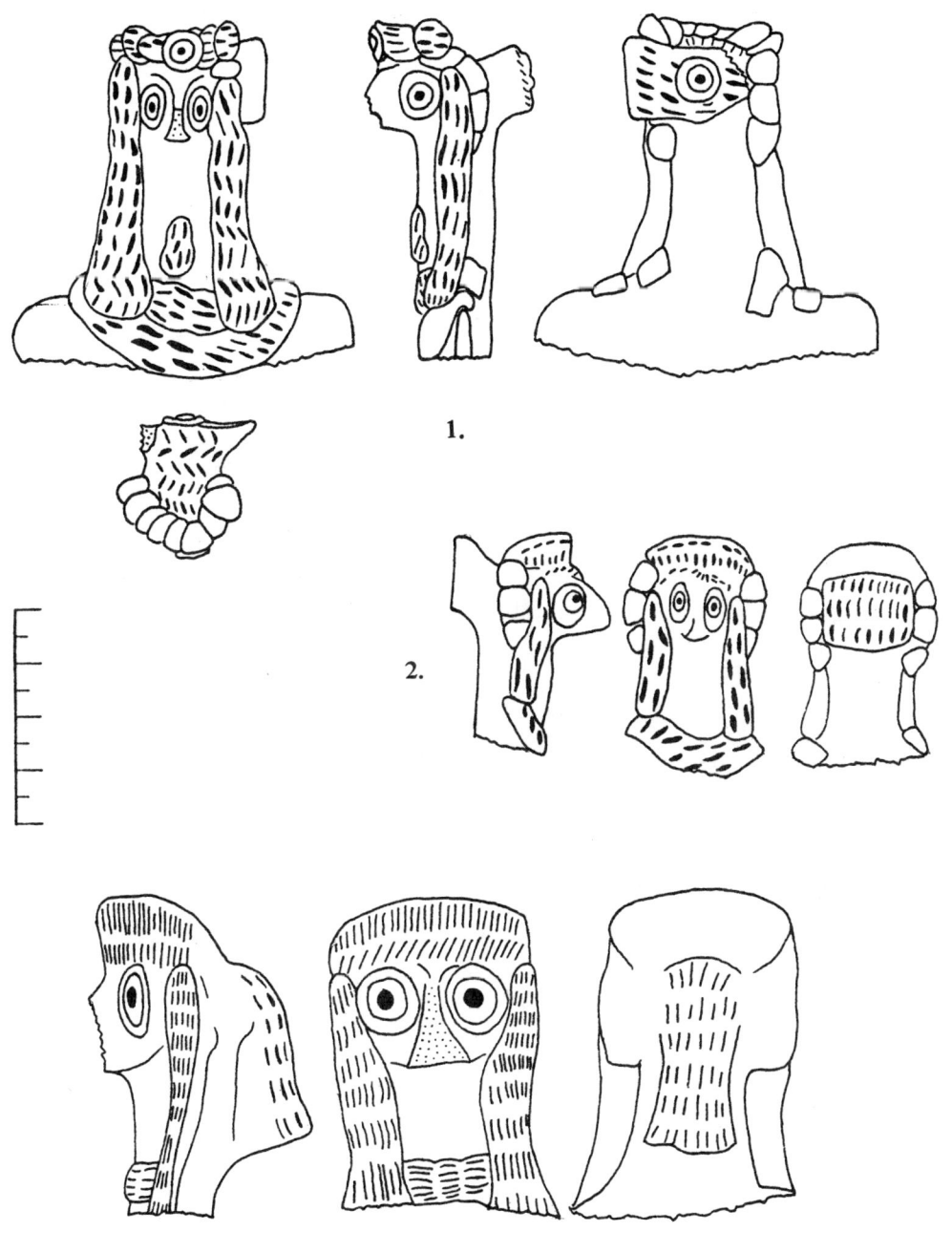

PLATE 3
Catalogue A

1. SLK 67-588, Type IA. Frontlet applied to the crown-like fringe, frontlet also applied to rectangular bun in back, small pendant at base of neck.

2. SLK 67-1082, Type IA. Bun with incisions representing hair.

3. SLK 67-998, Type IA. Choker necklace incised; pony tail incised.

PLATE 3A

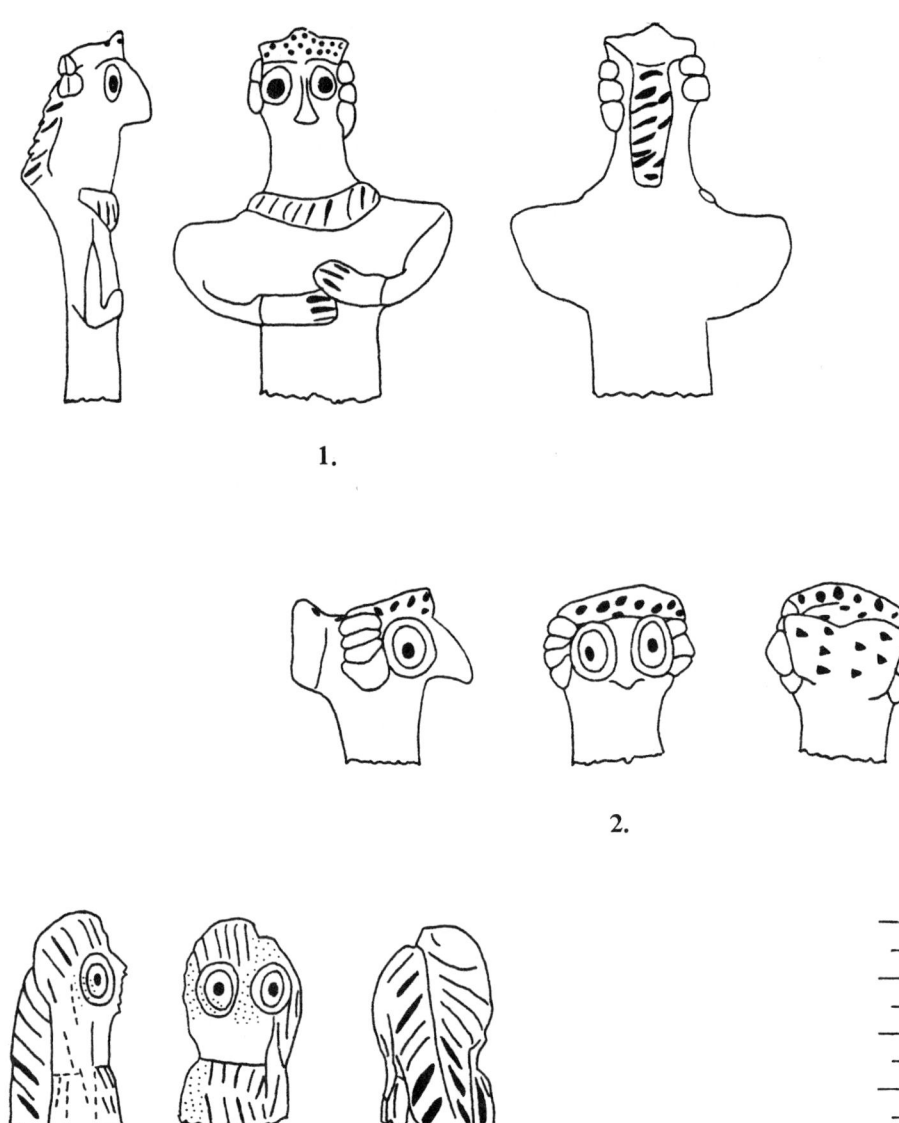

PLATE 3A
Catalogue A

1. SLK 67-146, Type IA. Dotted crown-like headdress, long diagonal incisions on pony tail.

2. SLK 67-939, Type IA. Crown-like headdress and bun, with dot decoration. Dot decoration also on top of head and back of crown headdress.

3. SLK 67-944, Type IA. Crown with vertically incised lines, double necklace at neck, vertical incised lines. Pony tail incised with herringbone pattern.

PLATE 4

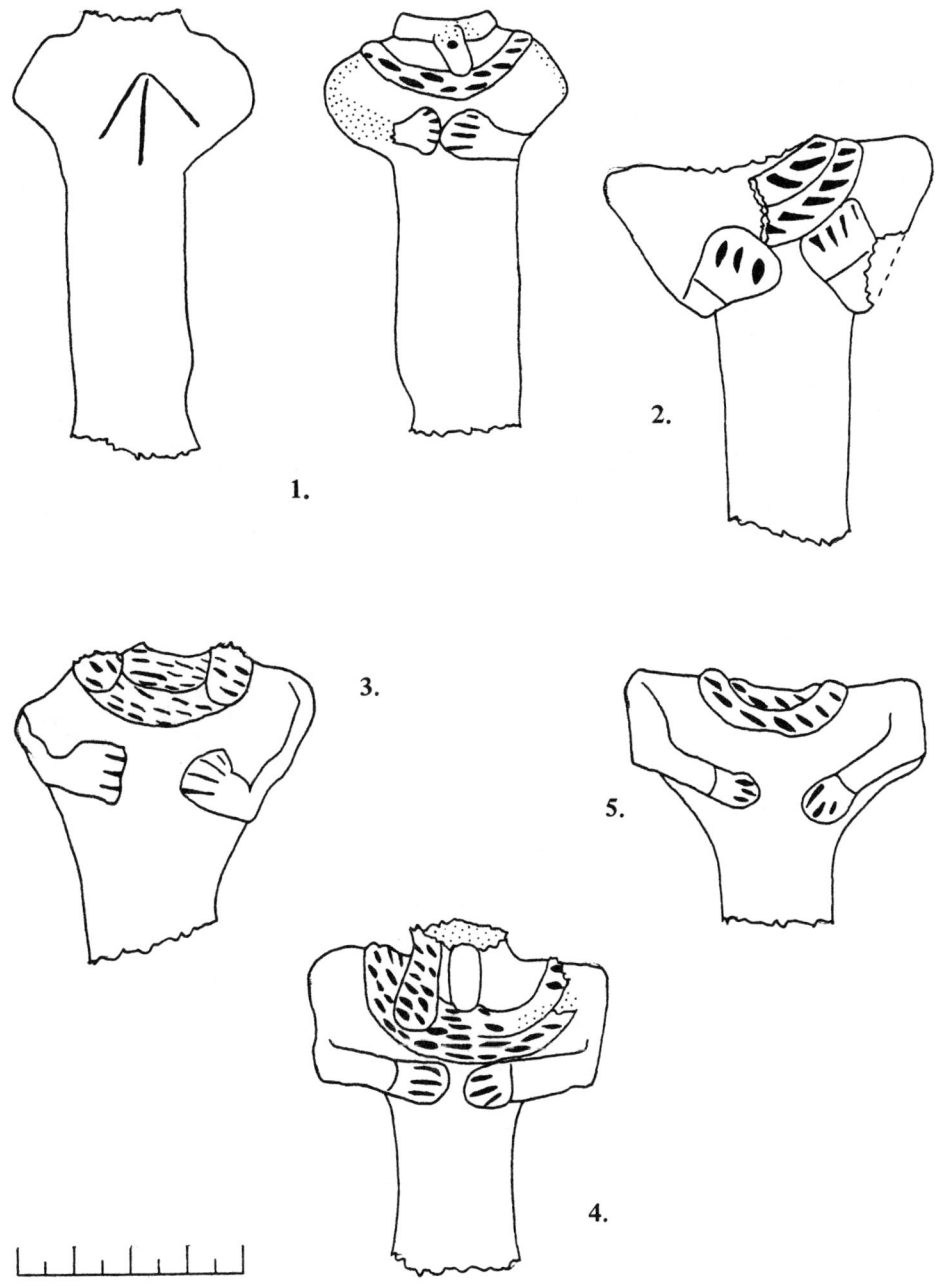

PLATE 4
Catalogue A

1. SLK 67-116, Type I. Remains of tassle between the two necklaces. Back has three incised lines between shoulders.

2. SLK 67-390, Type I. Forearms and large hands slant upward.

3. SLK 67-1272, Type I. Arms and hands carelessly applied to chest.

4. SLK 67-1125, Type I. Large pendant (?) at base of neck.

5. SLK 67-3, Type I. Forearms and hand slant downward.

PLATE 5

1.

2.

3.

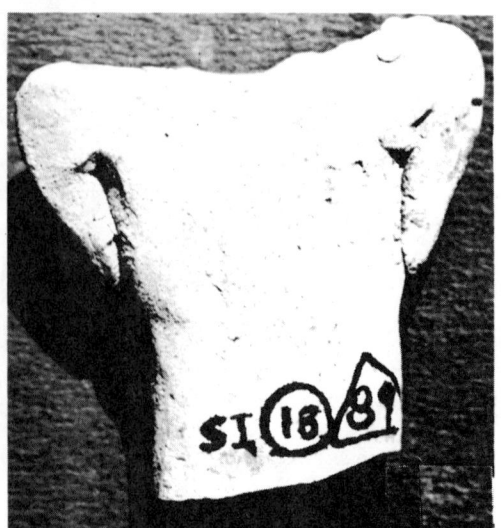

4.

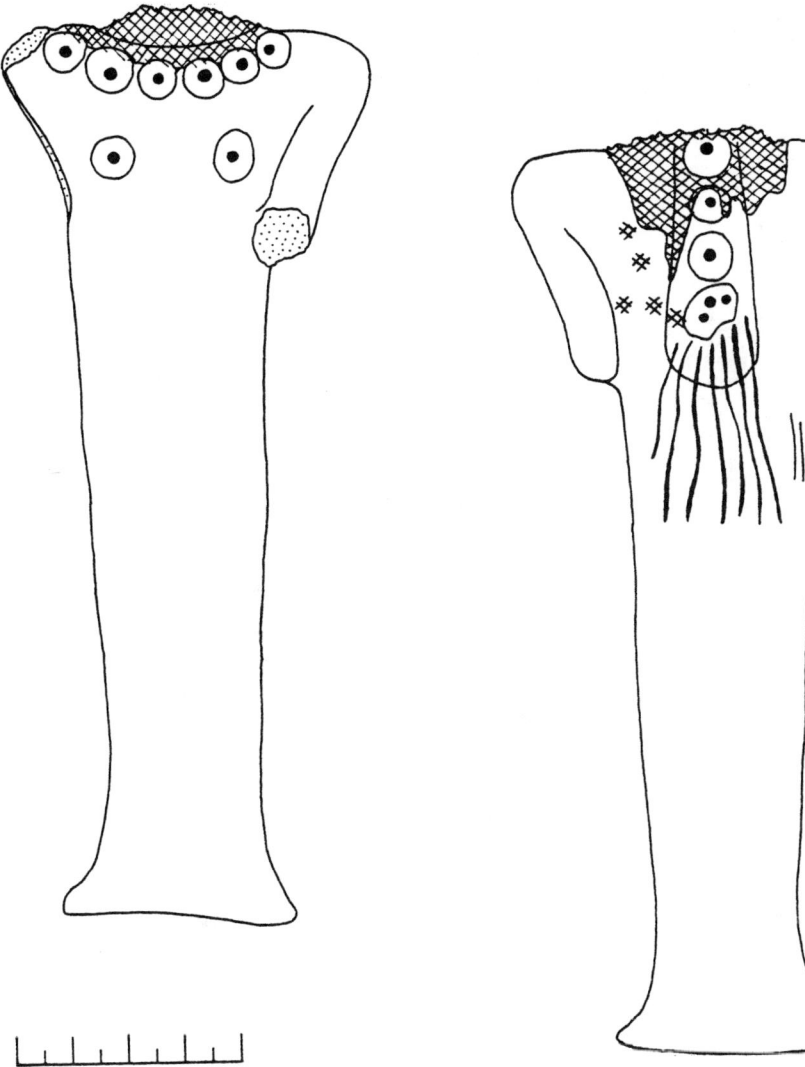

1.

PLATE 5
Catalogue A

1. SLK 67-207, Type IA. Large circular frontlet in center of crown, short pony tail behind.

2. SLK 67-595, Type IA. Long drop-shaped hair coils with dashes starting below ears, 2 holes in each ear. Plain long rectangular bun in back.

3. SI 1B 129, Type I. Prominent space between hands, forearms abbreviated.

4. SI 1B 89, Type I. Prominent space between hands, forearms absent.

PLATE 5A
Catalogue A

1. SLK 67-910, Type I. Applied pellet necklace, long pony tail with applied pellet and incised decorations; bitumen applied to necklace.

PLATE 6

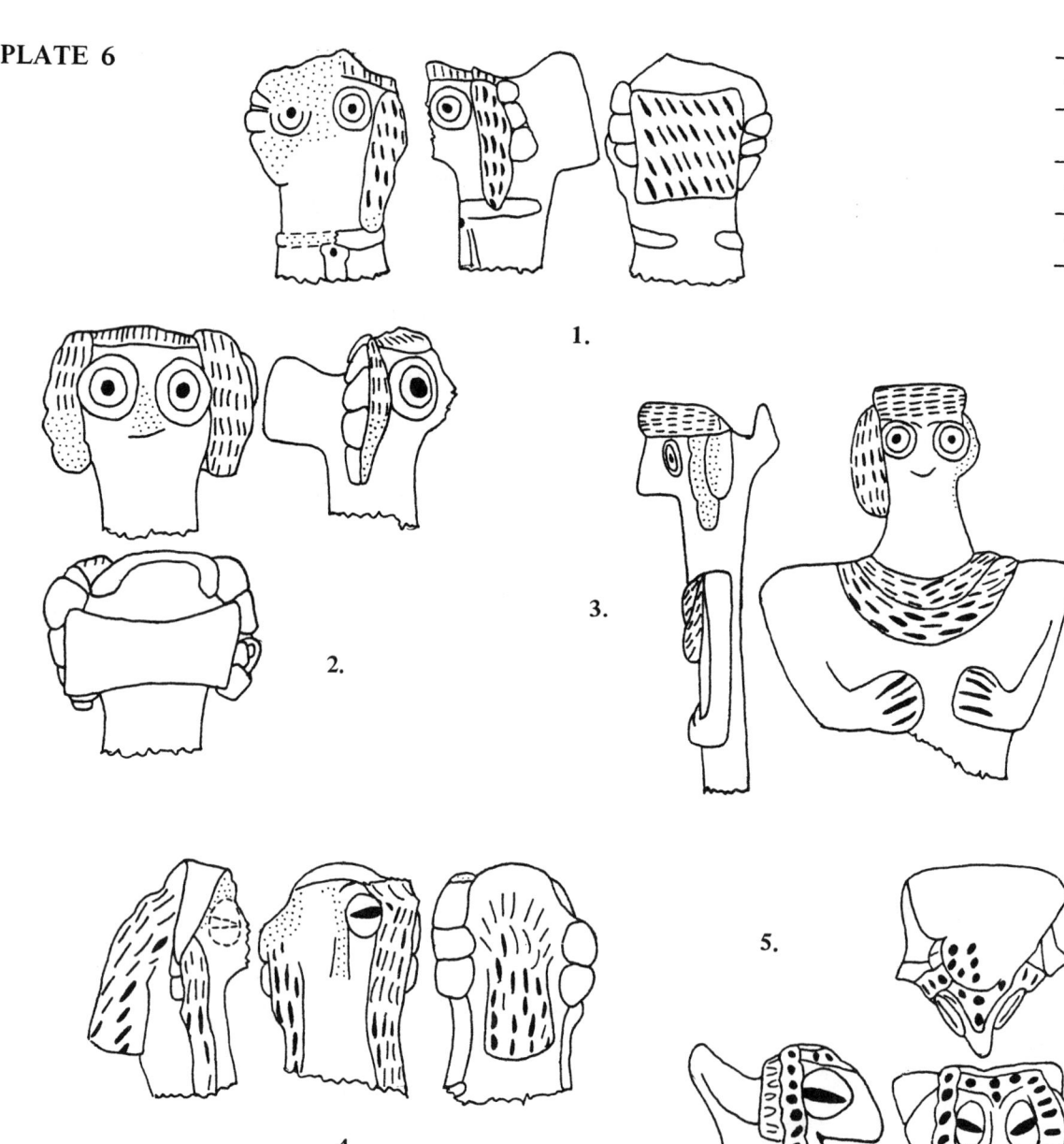

PLATE 6
Catalogue A

1. SLK 67-676, Type IB. Bun at back with 4 rows of diagonal dashes.

2. SLK 67-525, Type IB. Flat crown with vertical dashes. Short hair coils, large, rectangular undecorated bun.

3. SLK 67-1000, Type IB. Undecorated bun at back.

4. SLK 67-564, Type IC. Applied dot and dash eyes. Pony tail.

5. SLK 67-638, Type IC. Incised mouth with archaic smile, short, wide incisions on side curls; crown and parts of top of head decorated with punctuate dots; applied pellet eyes diagonally slashed; bun behind.

PLATE 7

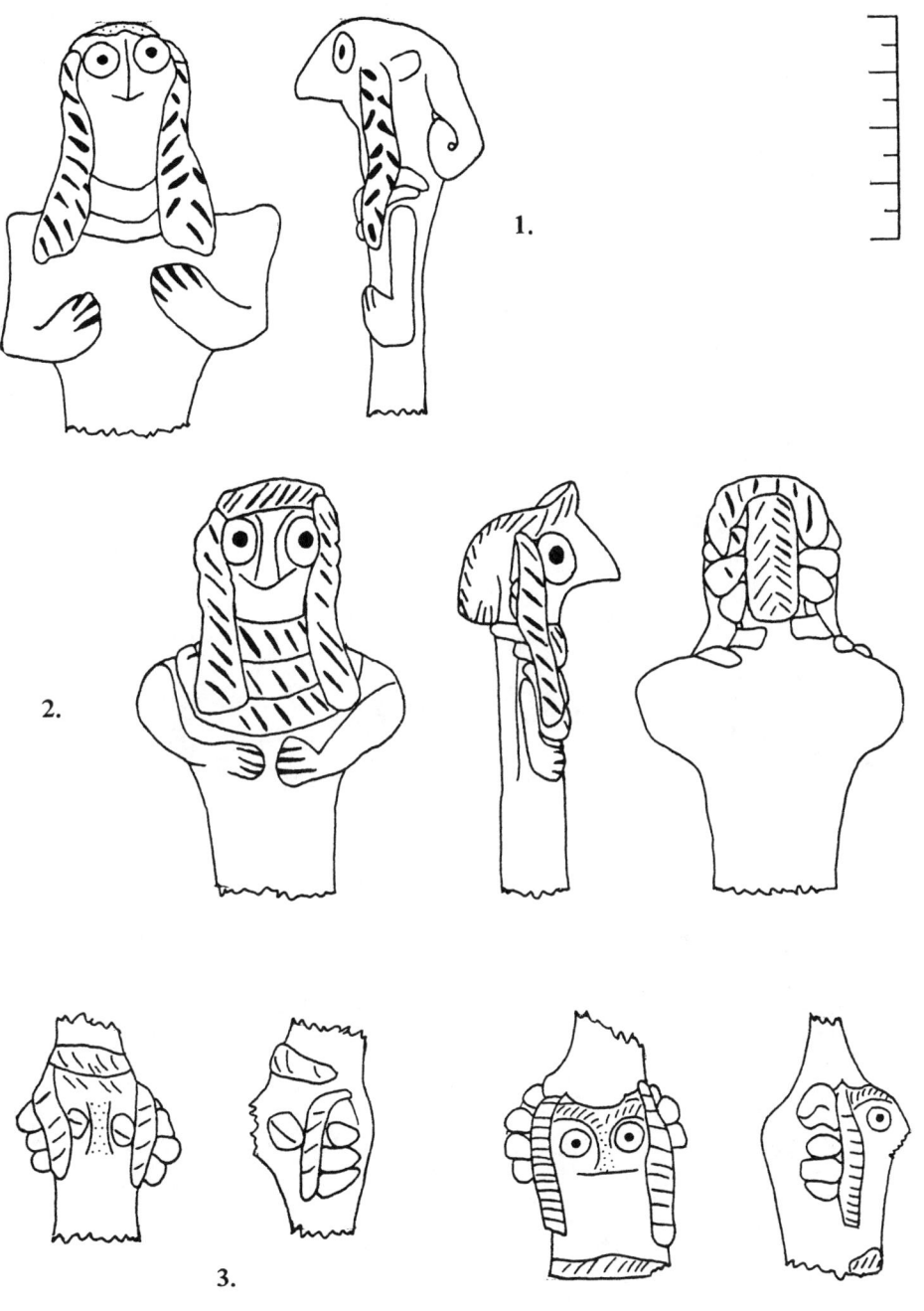

PLATE 7
Catalogue A

1. SLK 67-607, Type ID. Undecorated pony tail curled under.

2. SLK 67-392, Type ID. Perforated between neck and hair curls.

3. SLK 67-952, Type IE. Applied pellet eyes with diagonal slashes.

4. SLK 67-382, Type IE. Tall broken headdress, eyebrows of applied bands with incisions.

PLATE 7A

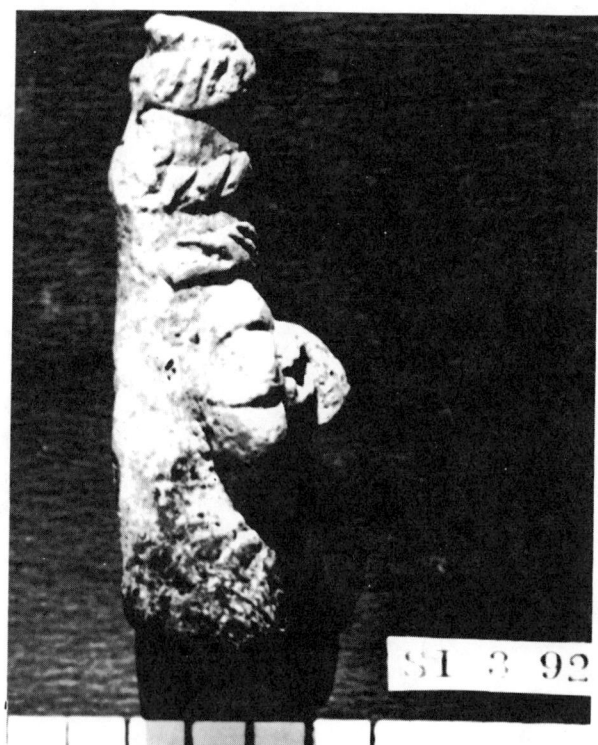

1.

PLATE 7B

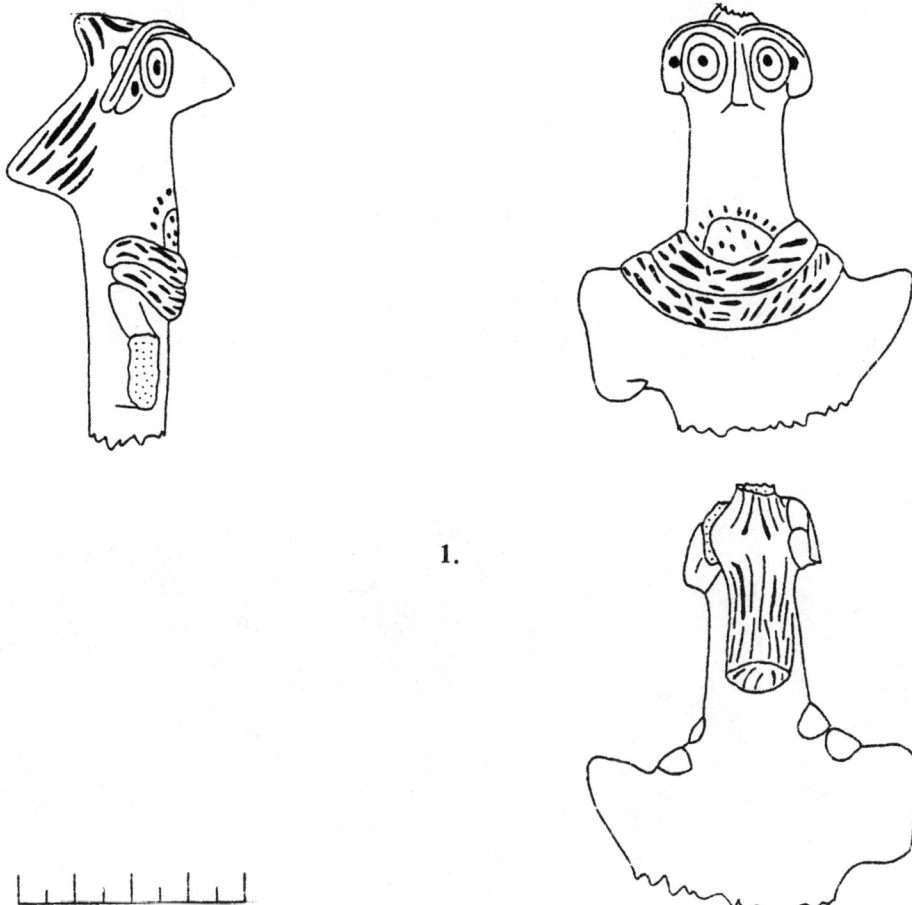

1.

PLATE 7A
Catalogue A

1. SI 3 92, Type IE. Tall columnar headdress with 3 horizontally applied bands; no tresses, back of head plain.

PLATE 7B
Catalogue A

1. SLK 67-930, Type IF. Arc-shaped, incised and stippled decoration above necklace; prominent eyebrows.

PLATE 8

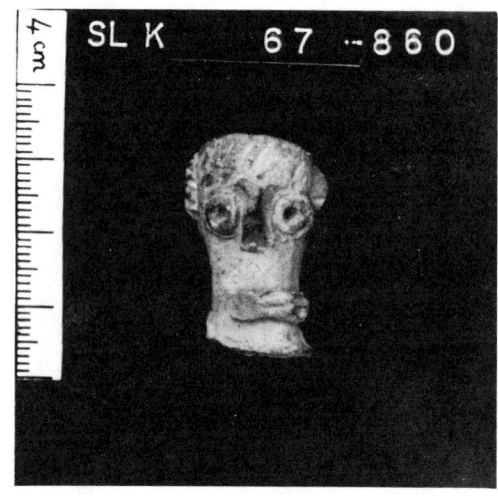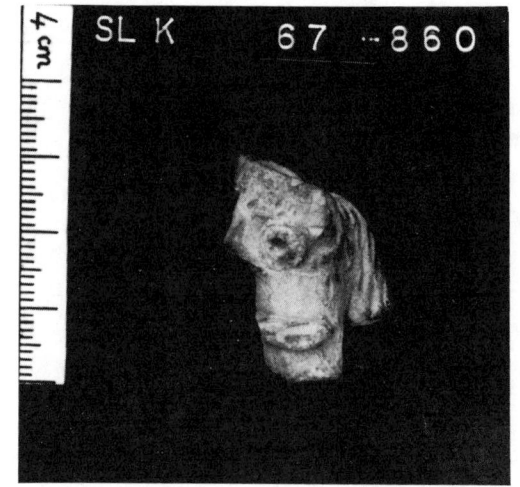

1.

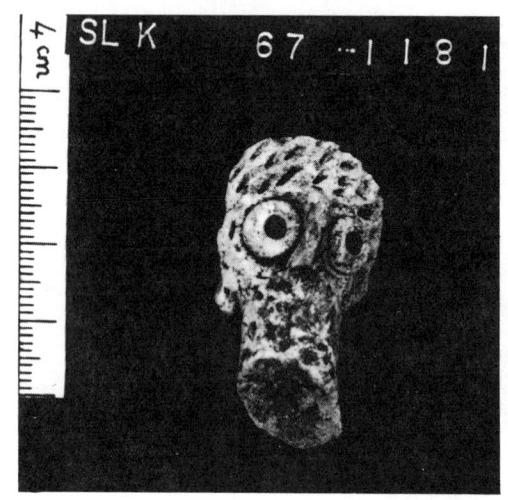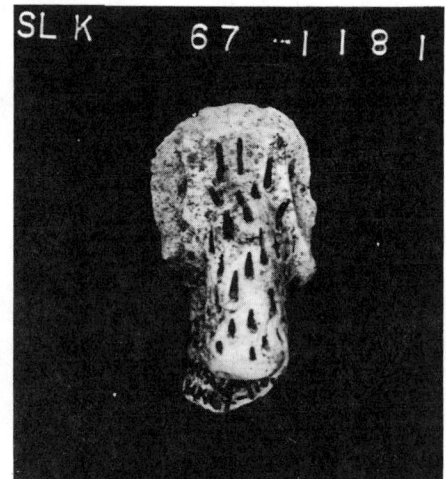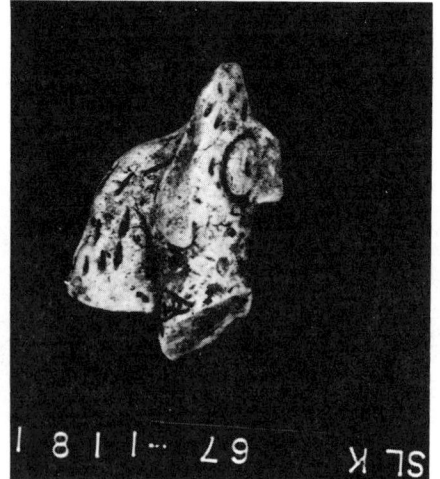

2.

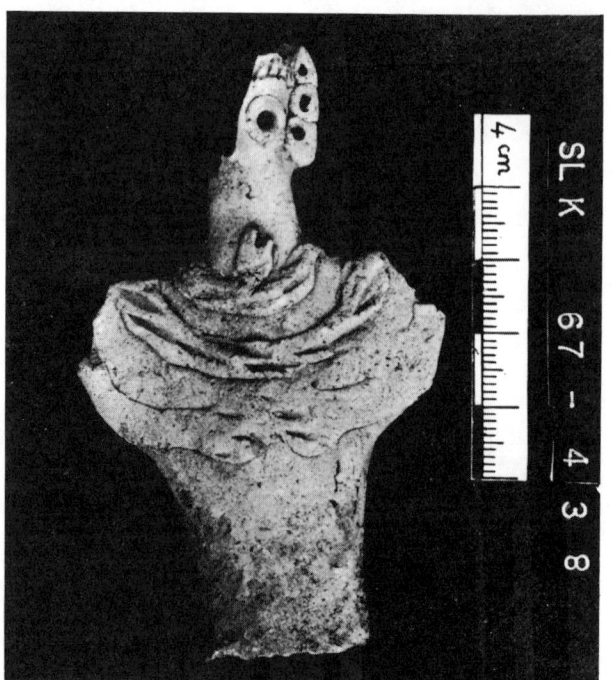

3.

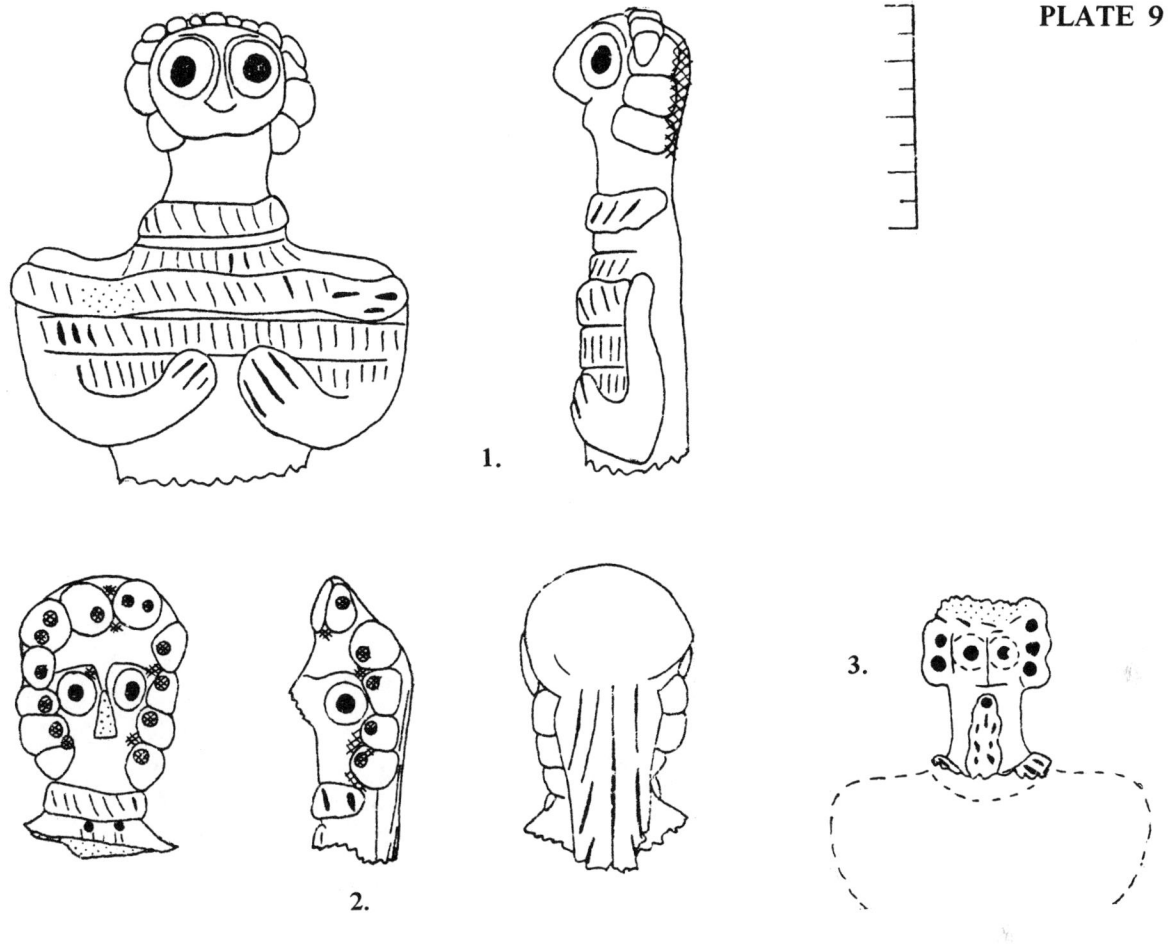

PLATE 8
Catalogue A

1. SLK 67-860, Type IF. Badly worn.

2. SLK 67-1181, Type IF. Edges of headdress broken; slight tilt to the head; pony tail.

3. SLK 67-438, Type IH. Pincurls at each side of the face; pendant (?) above upper strand of the necklace; arms in low relief.

PLATE 9
Catalogue A

1. SLK 67-945, Type IG. Necklace at base of neck and applied bands across shoulders; bitumen applied to back of head, arms curl up slightly.

2. SLK 67-1174, Type IJ. Crown headdress with applied and punctured pellets replacing tresses; choker necklace with diagonal incisions and 2 tassels (?); remains of bitumen on headdress, hair curls, and around eyes.

3. SLK 67-180, Type I. Broken crown headdress; punctuated eyes; ear flaps with 3 vertically aligned perforations; large pendant descends from below mouth; remains of short pony tail.

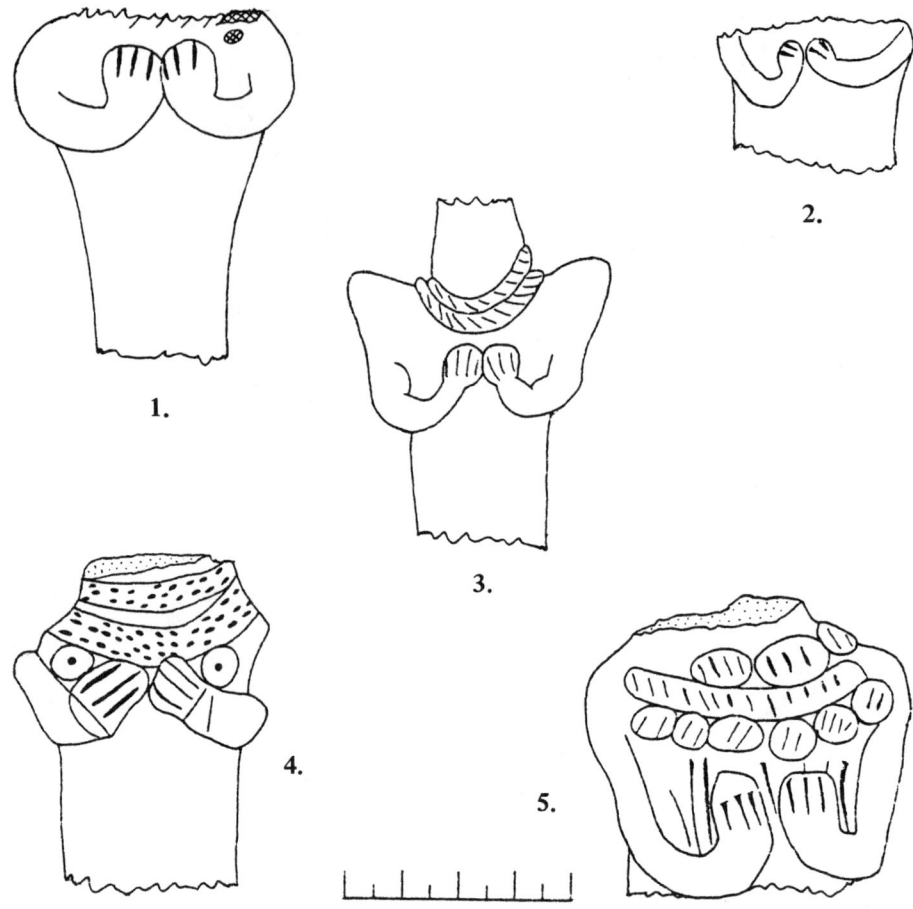

PLATE 10
Catalogue A

1. SLK 67-425, Type II. Traces of bitumen at base of neck.

2. SLK 67-19, Type II. Arms which curve upward carelessly applied.

3. SLK 67-79, Type II. No trace of tresses at sides of neck.

4. SLK 67-477, Type II. Hands with 2 incisions on wrists curve upward between the applied pellet breasts.

5. SLK 67-666, Type II. Elaborate single strand necklace with attached pendants (?) above and below; grooves on chest upon which applied arms and hands curve upward.

PLATE 11
Catalogue A

1. SLK 67-635, Type II. Bitumen applied to top of shoulder in antiquity to repair break; arms crudely applied to chest.

2. SLK 67-155, Type II. One applied pellet breast preserved.

3. SLK 67-1245, Type II. Small arm curves up around preserved pellet breast.

4. SLK 67-11, Type II. Arms curve upward between applied and punctured pellet breasts.

5. SI 1B 43, Type II. Upward curving hands exceptionally large.

PLATE 11

1.

2.

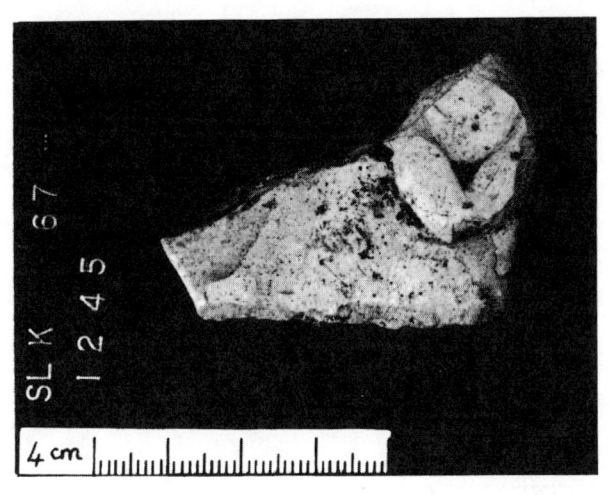

3.

4.

5.

PLATE 12
Catalogue A

1. SLK 67-695, Type IV. Conical headdress broken at top; oval-shaped applied eyes; applied eyebrows; horizontal ridge at back of head; bitumen applied to break at waist.

2. SLK 67-1128, Type IV. Oval-shaped applied eyes, applied eyebrows.

3. SLK 67-391, Type III. Bearded figure with hairy chest.

4. WRD 67-1, Type V. Neck to waist.

5. SLK 67-531, Type V. Bitumen applied to broken surfaces, to back of head, to forehead and necklace area.

6. SLK 67-623, Type V. Incised eyebrows.

7. SLK 67-2, untyped. Figurine with male, conical headdress, and with arms positioned as female figurines.

PLATE 12

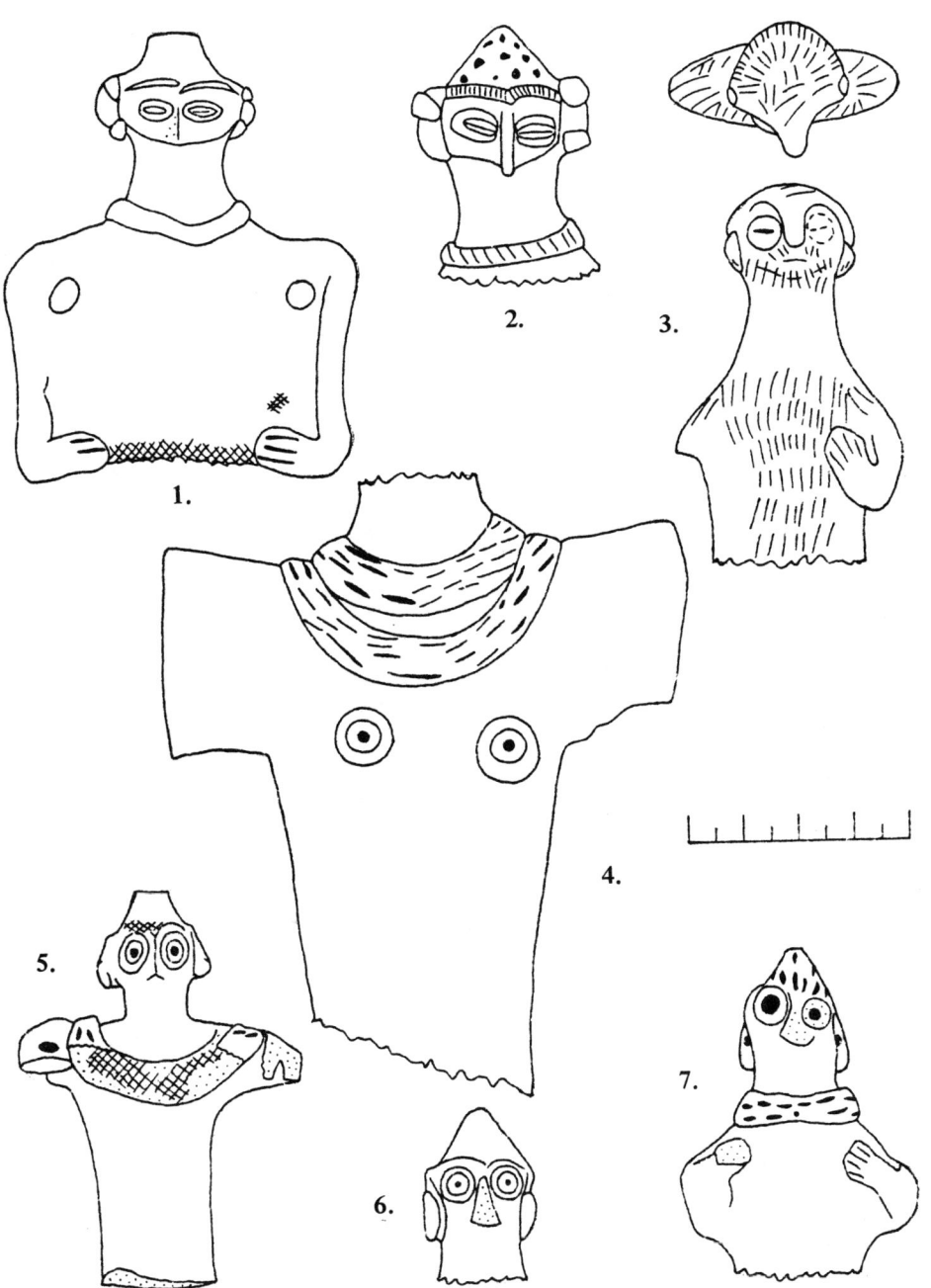

PLATE 13
Catalogue A

1. SLK 67-704, Type V. Stubby projecting arms vertically perforated; oval, slightly concave base.

2. SLK 67-1123, Type V. Vertically pierced stubby arms project from elbow; joins head SLK 67-1085.

3. SLK 67-633, Type V. Arm Stumps vertically pierced.

4. SLK 67-993, Type V. One applied breast, 1 long necklace above breast near "armpit"; arm lost, but probably projected forward; back has pony tail from which incised lines radiate.

5. SI 1B 63, Type V. Arm stumps vertically pierced; vertical incisions on torso.

6. SI 1B 93, Type V. Tapering torso with insubstantial arm stumps.

PLATE 13

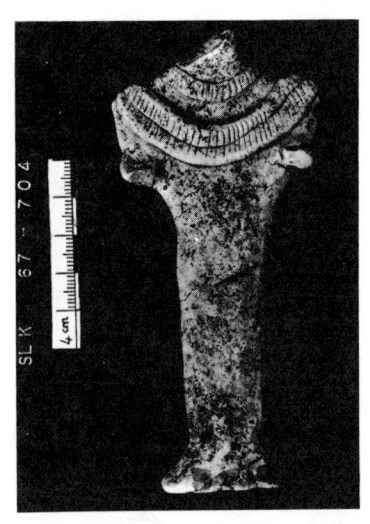

1.

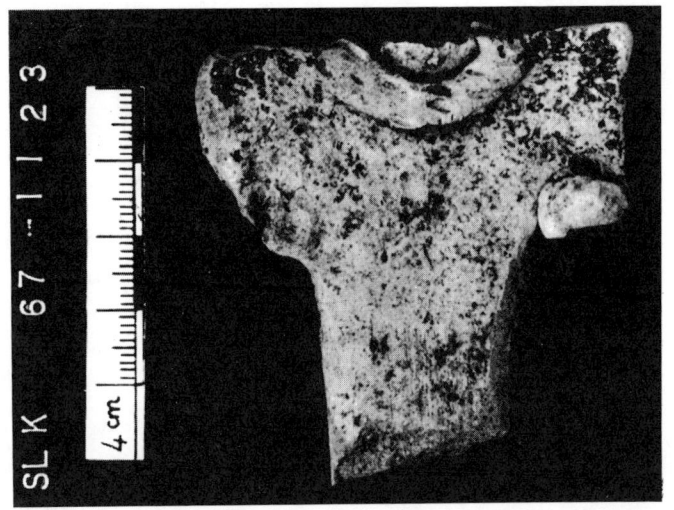

2.

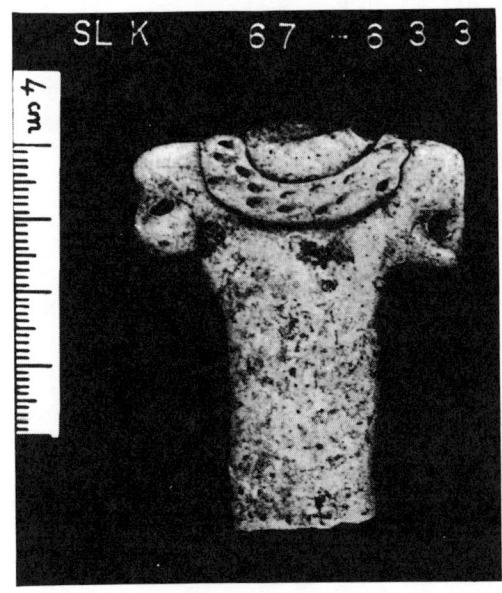

3.

4.

5.

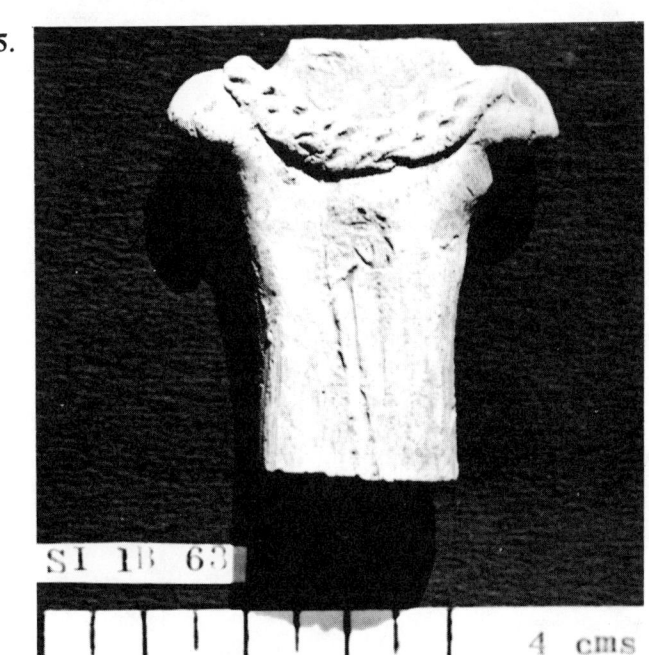

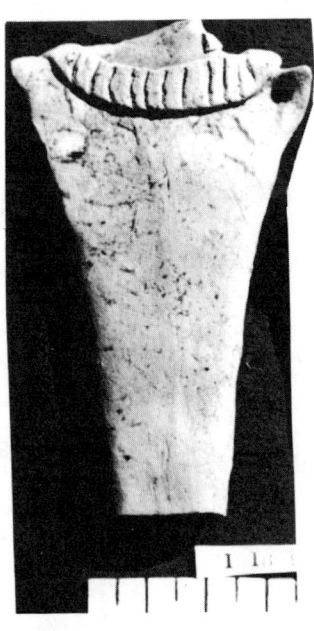

6.

PLATE 14
Catalogue A

1. SI 1B 109, Type V. Upper body.

2. SLK 67-960, Type V. Vertical perforations in arm stumps.

3. SLK 67-978, Type V. Hole in top of extended arm stumps.

4. SI 1B 12, Type V. Perforated arm stump, vertical incisions on chest.

5. SLK 67-1253, Type V. Arm stumps not perforated, extended forward.

6. SLK 67-904, Type V. Short arms extended from elbow; rounded shoulders.

PLATE 14

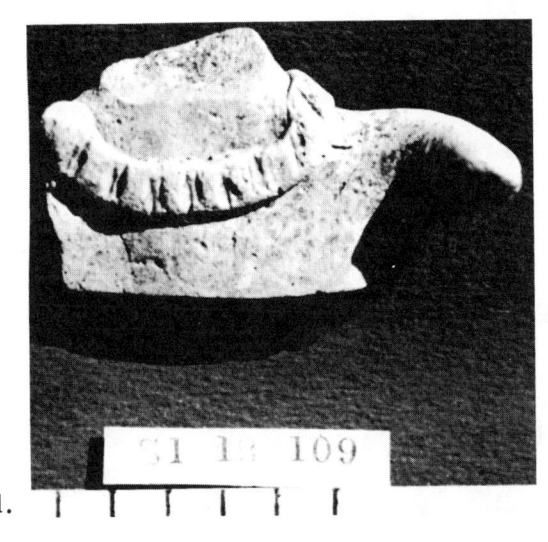

1.

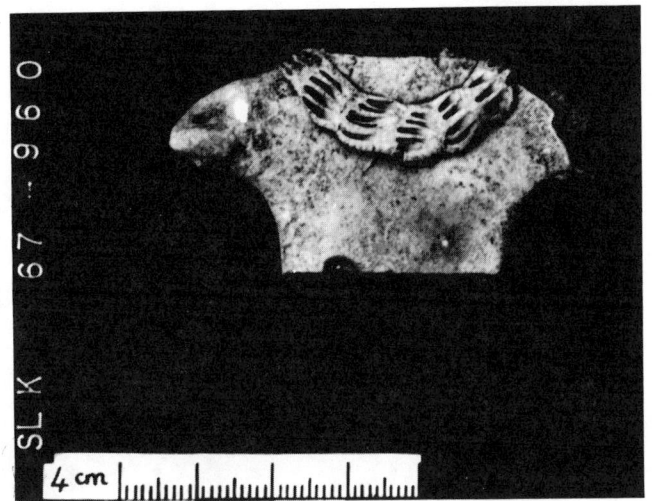

2.

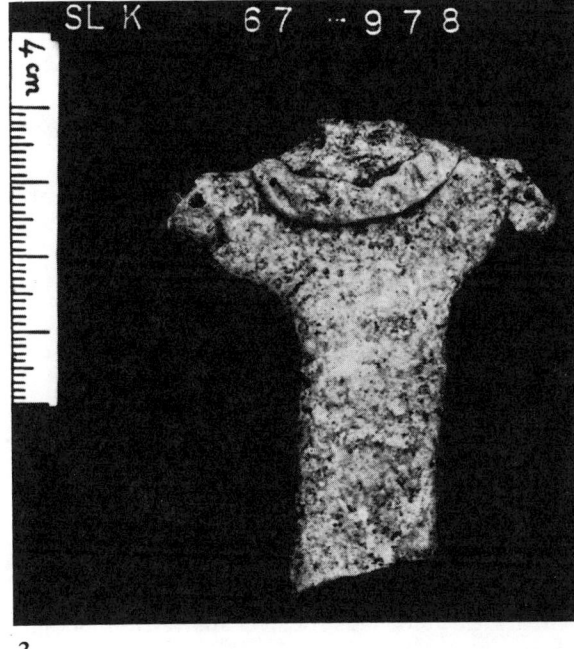

3.

4.

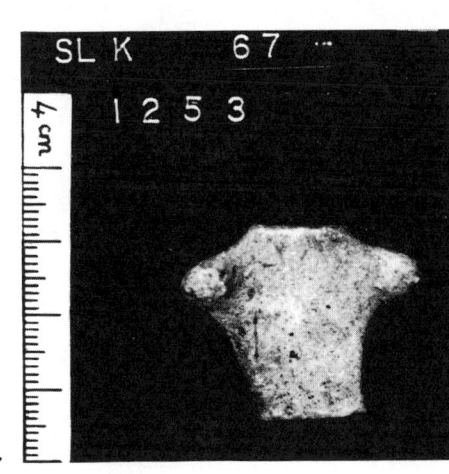

5.

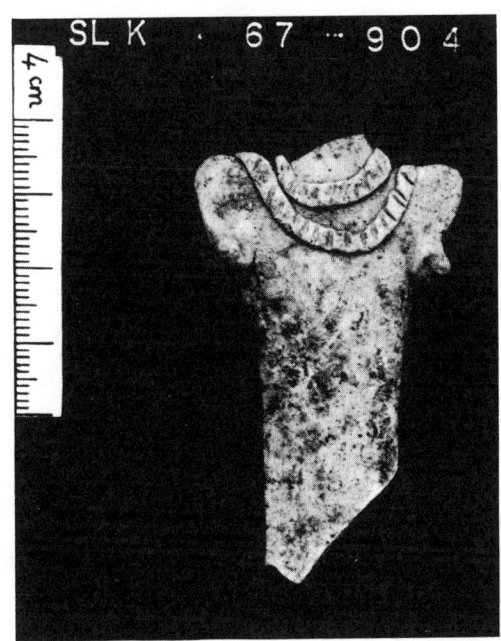

6.

PLATE 15
Catalogue B

1. WRD 67-2, Type V. Torso incised with contiguous triangles and vertical incisions topped by a horizontal incision.

Catalog A

2. SLK 67-938, Type V. Torso incised with contiguous triangles and vertical incisions topped by a horizontal incision.

3. SLK 67-144, Type V. Four horizontally aligned triangles.

4. SLK 67-294, Type V. Torso incised with contiguous right triangles.

5. SLK 67-700, Type V. Incised axe (?)

6. SLK 67-1011, Type V. Applied pellets representing necklace with dangling pendants or beads.

7. SLK 67-1092, Type V. Arm stumps vertically pierced; chest incised with vertical parallel lines.

PLATE 15

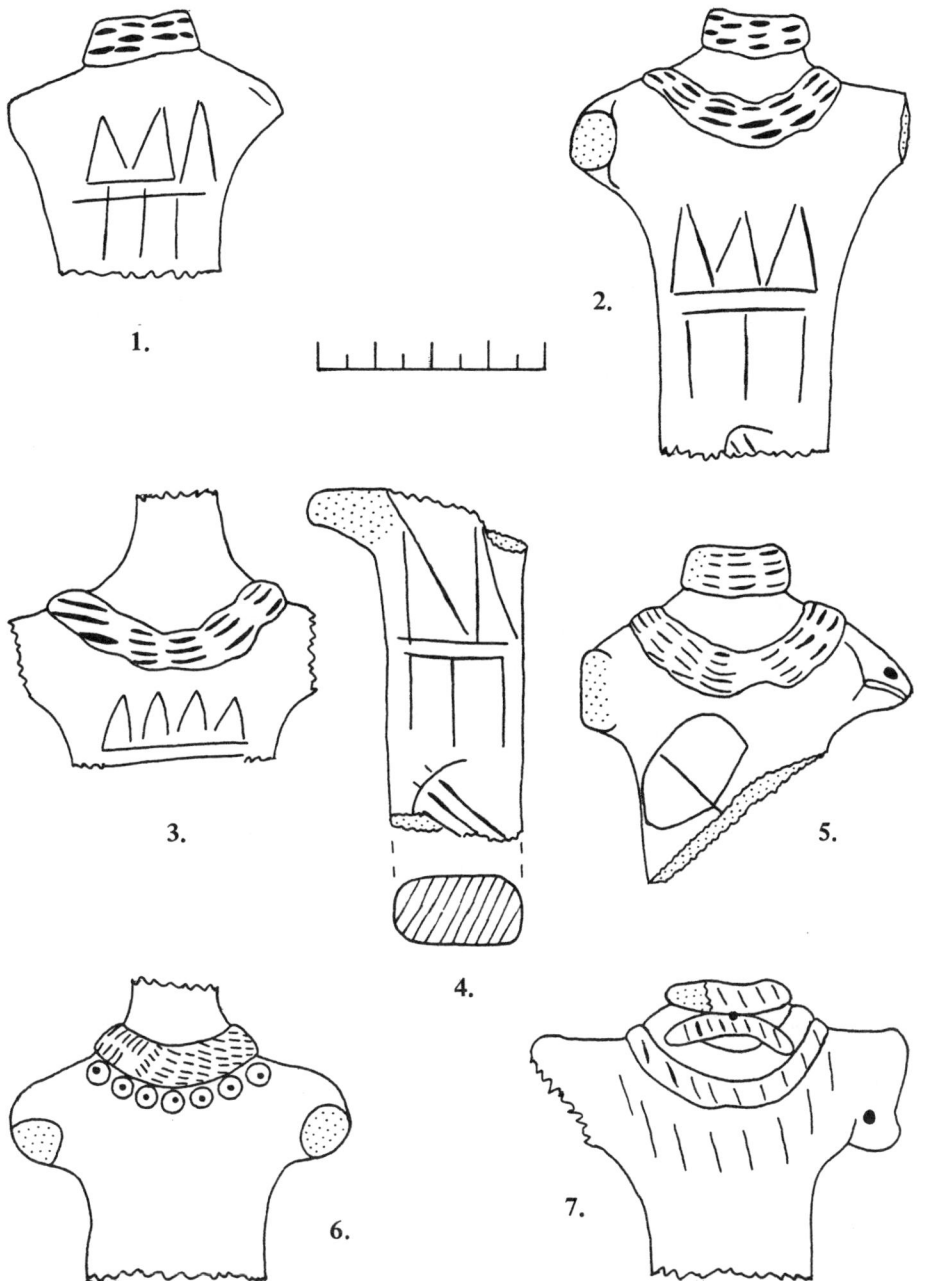

PLATE 16
Catalogue A

1. SLK 67-639, Type V. Tall conical headdress; incised eyebrows, single perforation in each ear lobe.

2. SLK 67-213, Type V. Conical headdress, perforated ears.

3. SLK 67-300, Type V. Conical headdress, perforated ears.

4. SI 1B 21, Type V. Conical headdress, perforated ears.

5. SLK 67-262, Type V. Conical headdress; perforated ears.

6. SI 1B 14, Type V. Head.

7. SLK 67-986, Type V. Ears not perforated; long neck.

8. SLK 67-859, Type V. Incised eyebrows; ears not perforated.

9. SLK 67-1085, Type V. Ears not perforated.

10. SLK 67-857, Type V. Conical headdress; ears perforated.

PLATE 16

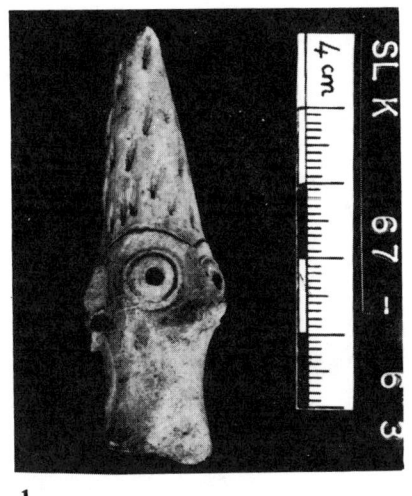
1.

2.

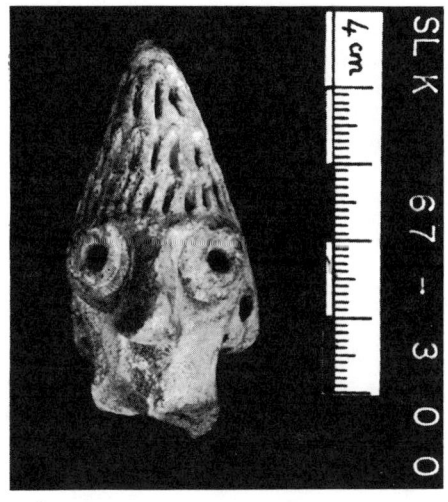
3.

4.

5.

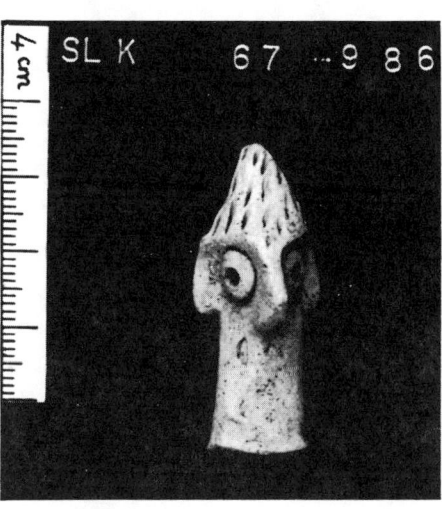
6.

7.

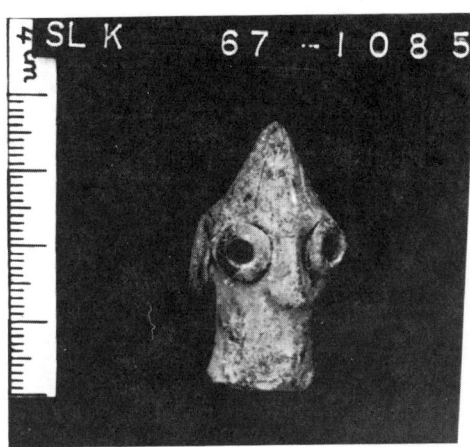
8.

9.

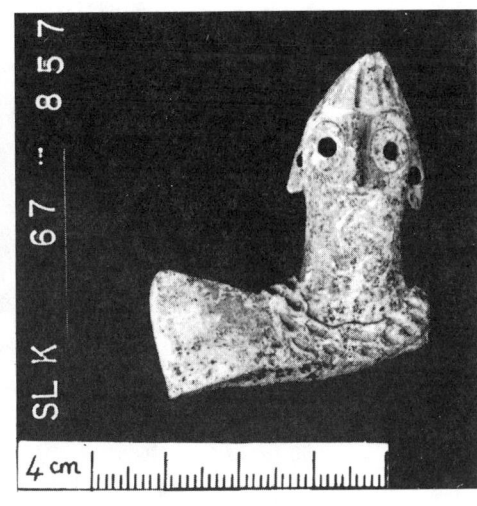
10.

PLATE 17
Catalogue A

1. SLK 67-214, Type VI. Partial perforation through surviving arm stump.

2. SLK 67-1032, Type VI. Single perforation in each arm stump.

3. WRD 67-31, Type VI. Well preserved arm stump not perforated.

4. SLK 67-681, Type VI. Hair on nape of neck indicated by incised lines.

PLATE 17

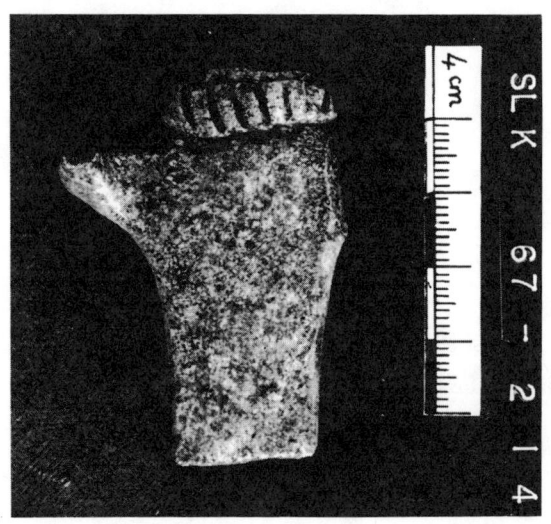

1.

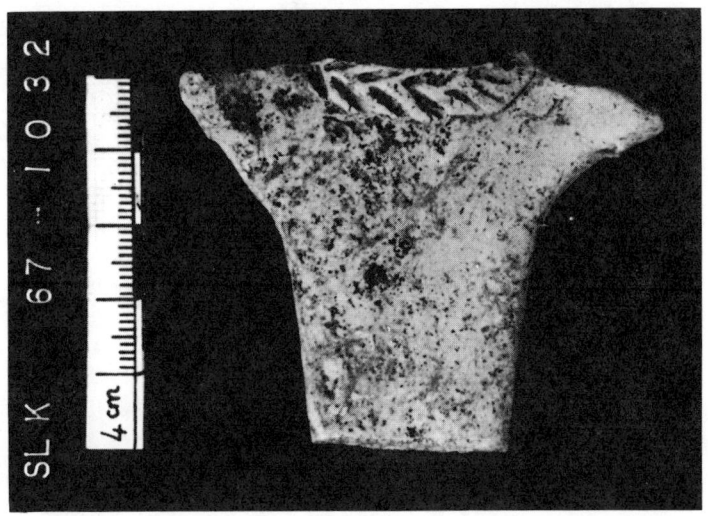

2.

3.

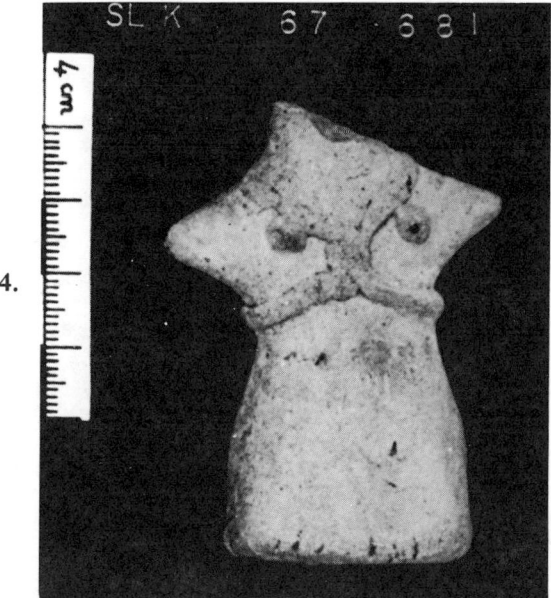

4.

PLATE 18
Catalogue A

1. S. Surf. 163, Type VII. Prongs of 4-pronged headdress broken away.

2. SI 1B 9, Type VII. Pellet folded over right ear.

3. SI 1B 61, Type VII. Applied pellet eyes with single diagonal slash in each.

4. SLK 67-620, Type VII. Tall, hollow headdress with 4 prongs, left ear broken, pellet folded over right ear.

5. SLK 67-399, Type VIII. Headdress hollow in center; "moustache" or ∧-shaped pendant.

6. SLK 67-479, Type VIII. Badly worn; vertical dashes on collar-type necklace.

PLATE 18

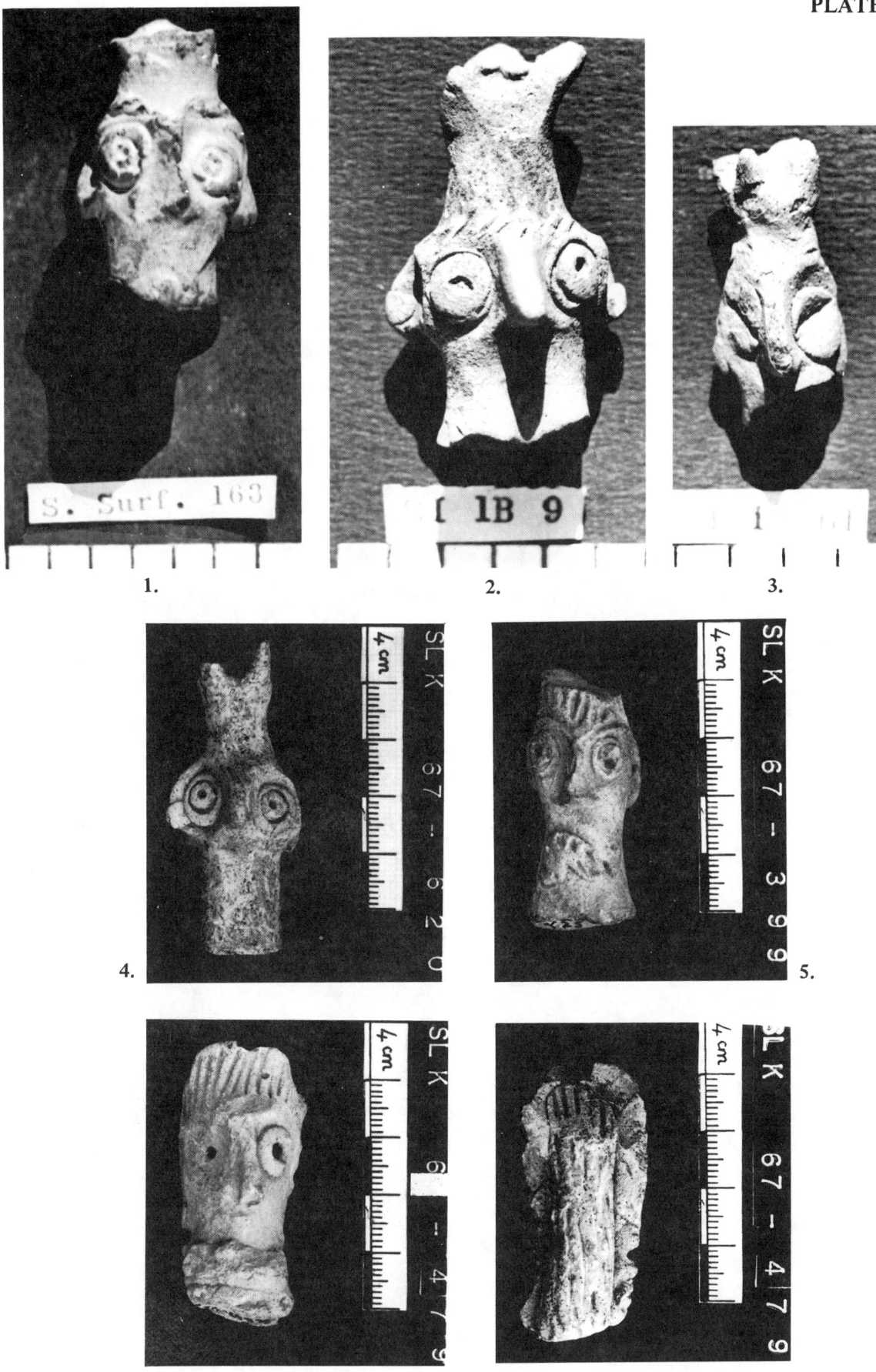

PLATE 19

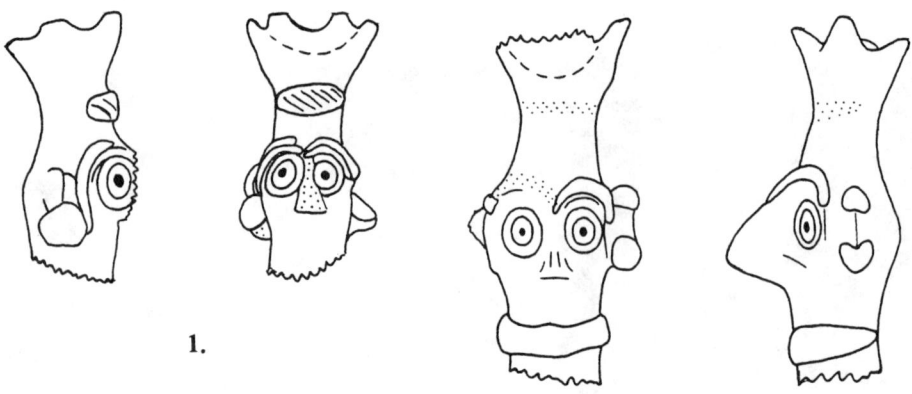

1.

2.

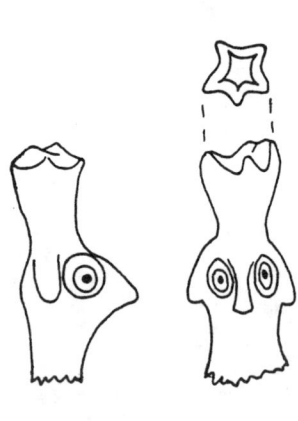

3.

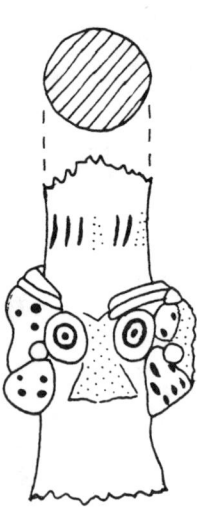

4.

PLATE 19
Catalogue A

1. SLK 67-1005, Type VII. Five-pronged headdress; horizontally aligned ears, prominent eyebrows of applied, curved strips.

2. SLK 67-422, Type VII. Four-pronged headdress; eyebrows of applied, curved strips of clay; left ear has pellet folded over top and bottom.

3. SLK 67-4, Type VII. Five-pronged headdress.

4. SLK 67-478, Type VII. Tall headdress, no secure evidence for prongs; prominent earflaps with central puncture in each.

PLATE 20

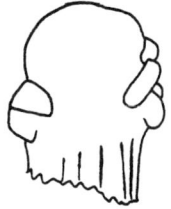  

1.

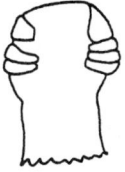  

2.

PLATE 20
Catalogue A

1. SLK 67-1132, Type IX. Beard and hair at nape of neck rendered by incisions.

2. SLK 67-1530, Type IX. Single pellet applied to left side of neck.

PLATE 21
Catalogue A

1. SI 2 68, Type X. Beard and hair at nape of neck rendered by irregular, vertical incisions.

2. SI 2 76, Type X. Applied pony tail.

3. SLK 67-1291, Type XII. Bitumen at break of legs; long hair coils, right one curled under at top.

4. SLK 67-897, Type XI. Hips and stubby legs of kilted figurine.

5. SLK 67-604, Type XIIIA. Broad splaying base.

6. SLK 67-1084, Type XIIIA. Broad splaying base.

7. SLK 67-493, Type XIIIA. Narrow base.

8. SLK 67-880, Type XIIIA. Narrow base.

PLATE 21

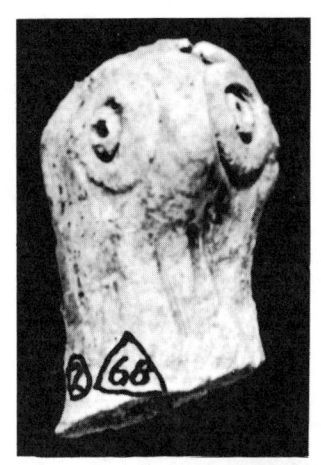

1.

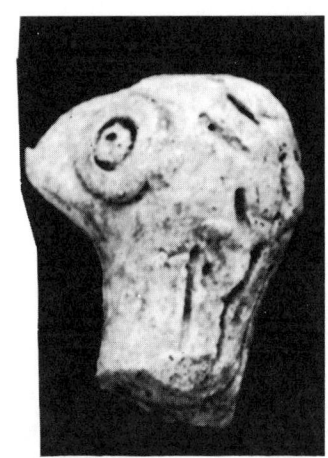

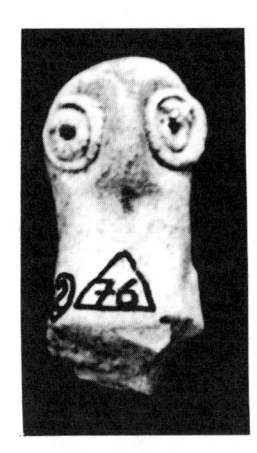

2.

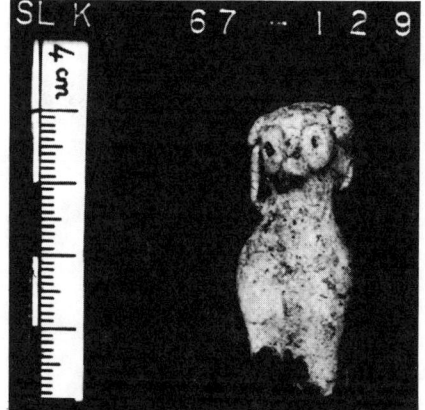

3.

4.

5.

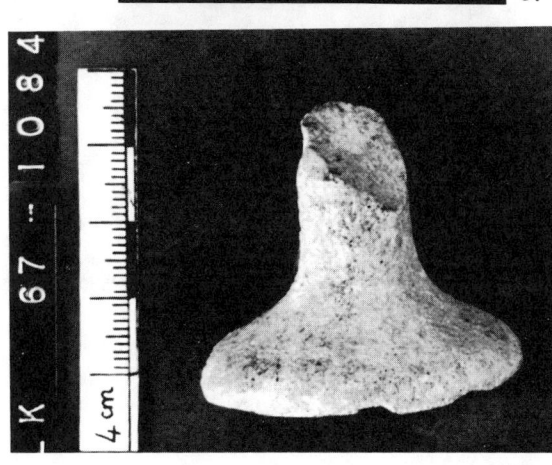

6.

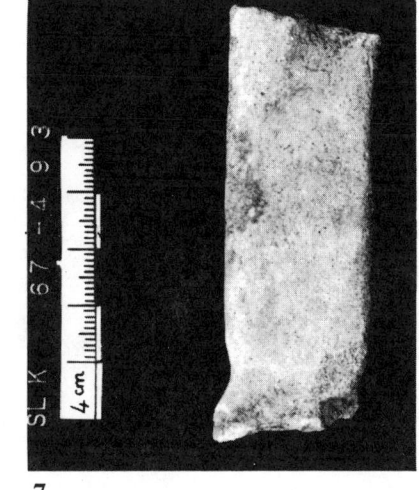

7.

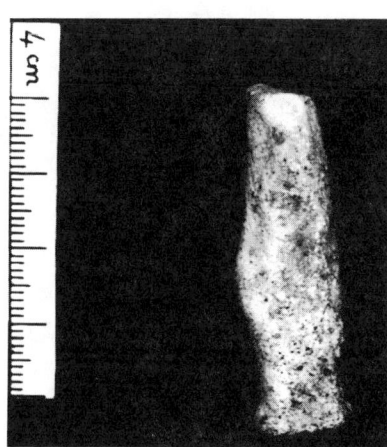

8.

PLATE 22
Catalogue A

1. SLK 67-378, Type XII. Torso hollow.

2. SLK 67-489, Type V. Complete except for head and left shoulder.

PLATE 22

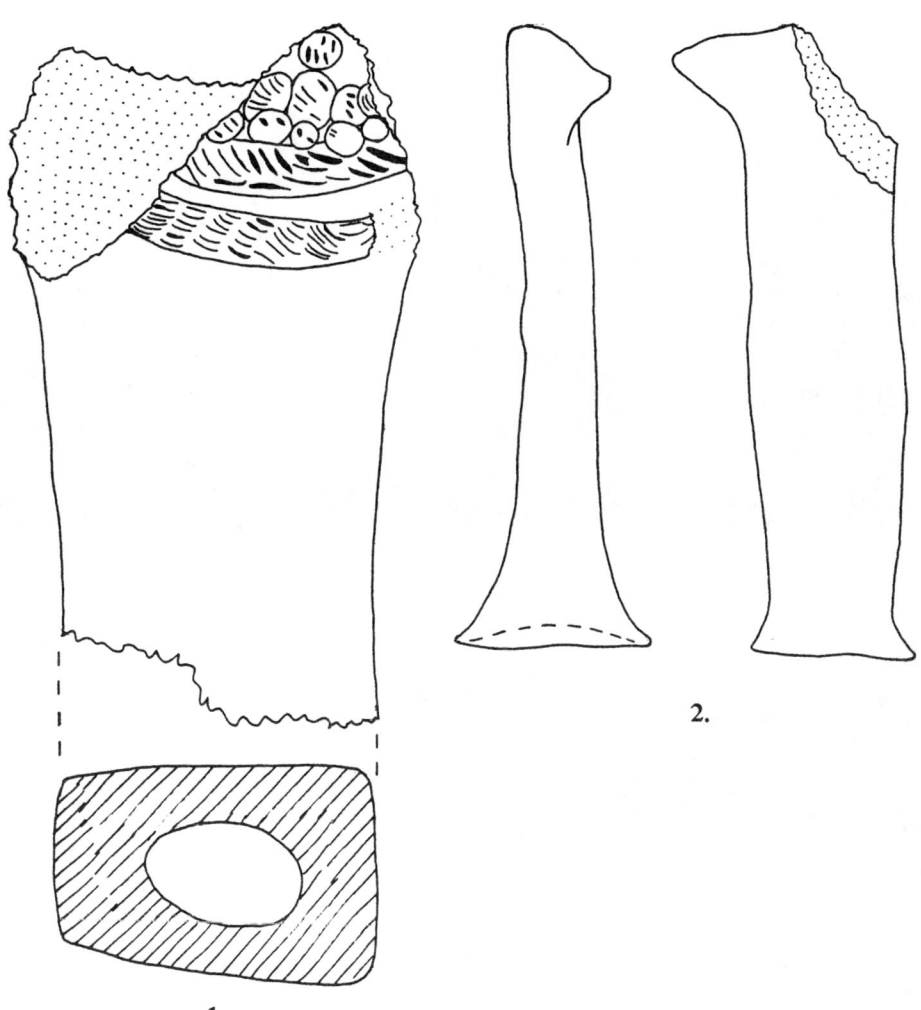

1.

2.

PLATE 23

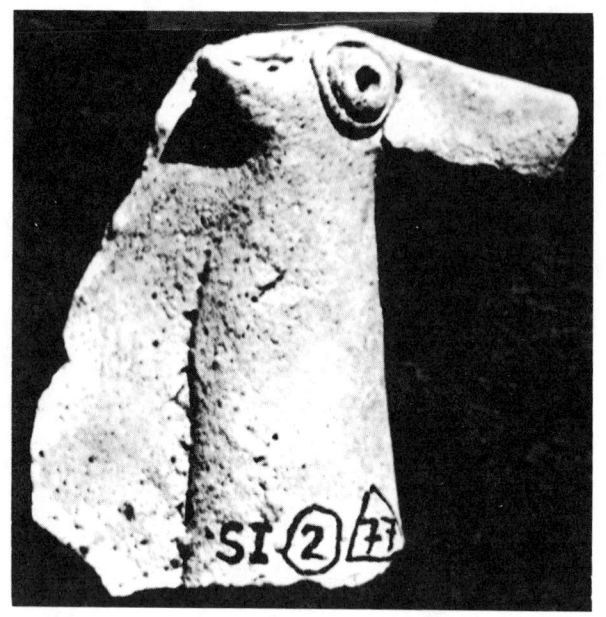
1.

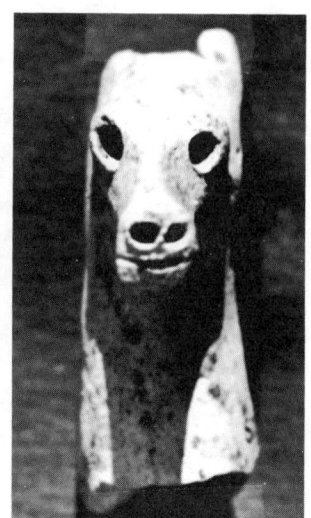
2.

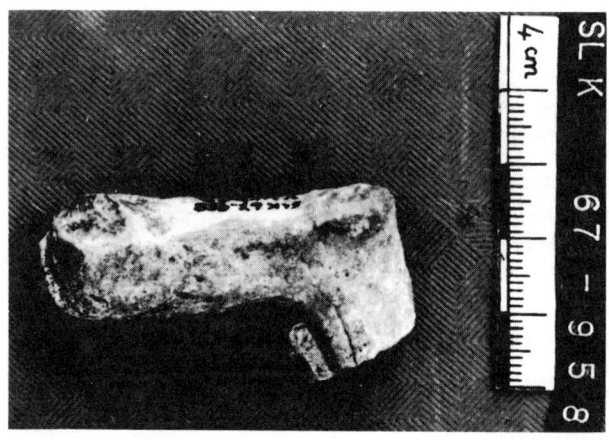
3.

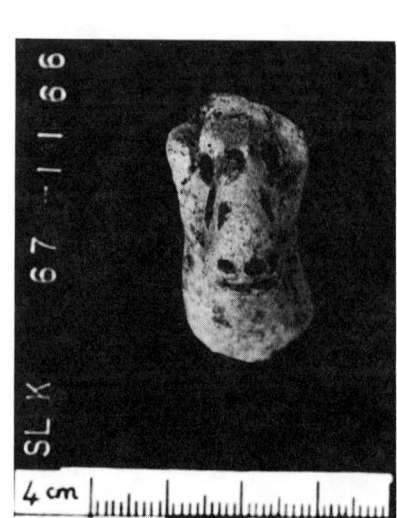
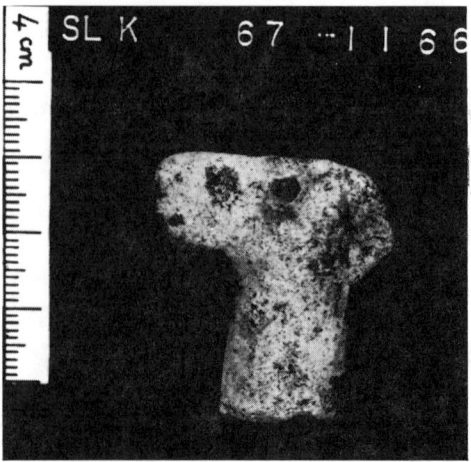
4.

PLATE 24

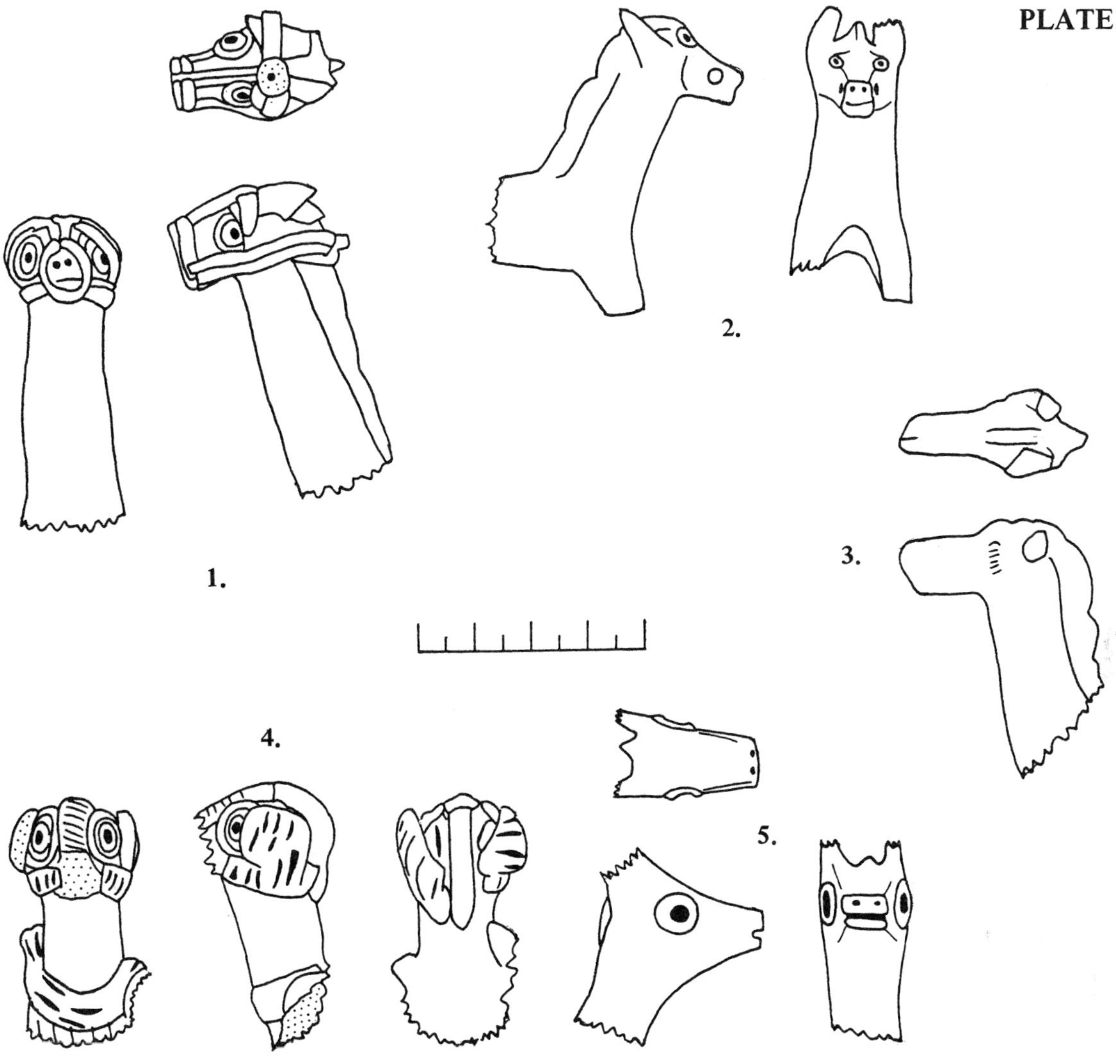

PLATE 23
Catalogue B

1. SI 2 77, horse? Prominent erect mane.

2. SI 2 75, horse? Prominent erect mane with diagonal incisions.

3. SLK 67-958, horse?

4. SLK 67-1166, equid? Rectangular muzzle.

PLATE 24
Catalogue B

1. SLK 67-936, horse. Long neck, erect mane, intact bridle.

2. SLK 67-295, horse. Hole in muzzle for bridle.

3. WRD 67-45, horse. Long neck with erect mane.

4. SLK 67-642, horse? Earflaps or blinkers cover part of each eye.

5. SLK 67-1109, horse? Slight ridge between broken ears may represent mane.

PLATE 25
Catalogue B

1. SI 1B 24, bull. Face; muzzle broken away.

2. SI 1B 52, bull. Face; muzzle broken away.

3. SI 2 102, bull. Face; muzzle and most of horns broken away.

4. SLK 67-503, bull. Face broken away.

5. SLK 67-152, bull. No features on face.

6. SLK 67-227, bull. Muzzle broken away; applied, punctured pellet eyes.

7. SLK 67-216, bull. Thin, tapering muzzle, eyes applied, punctured pellets.

PLATE 25

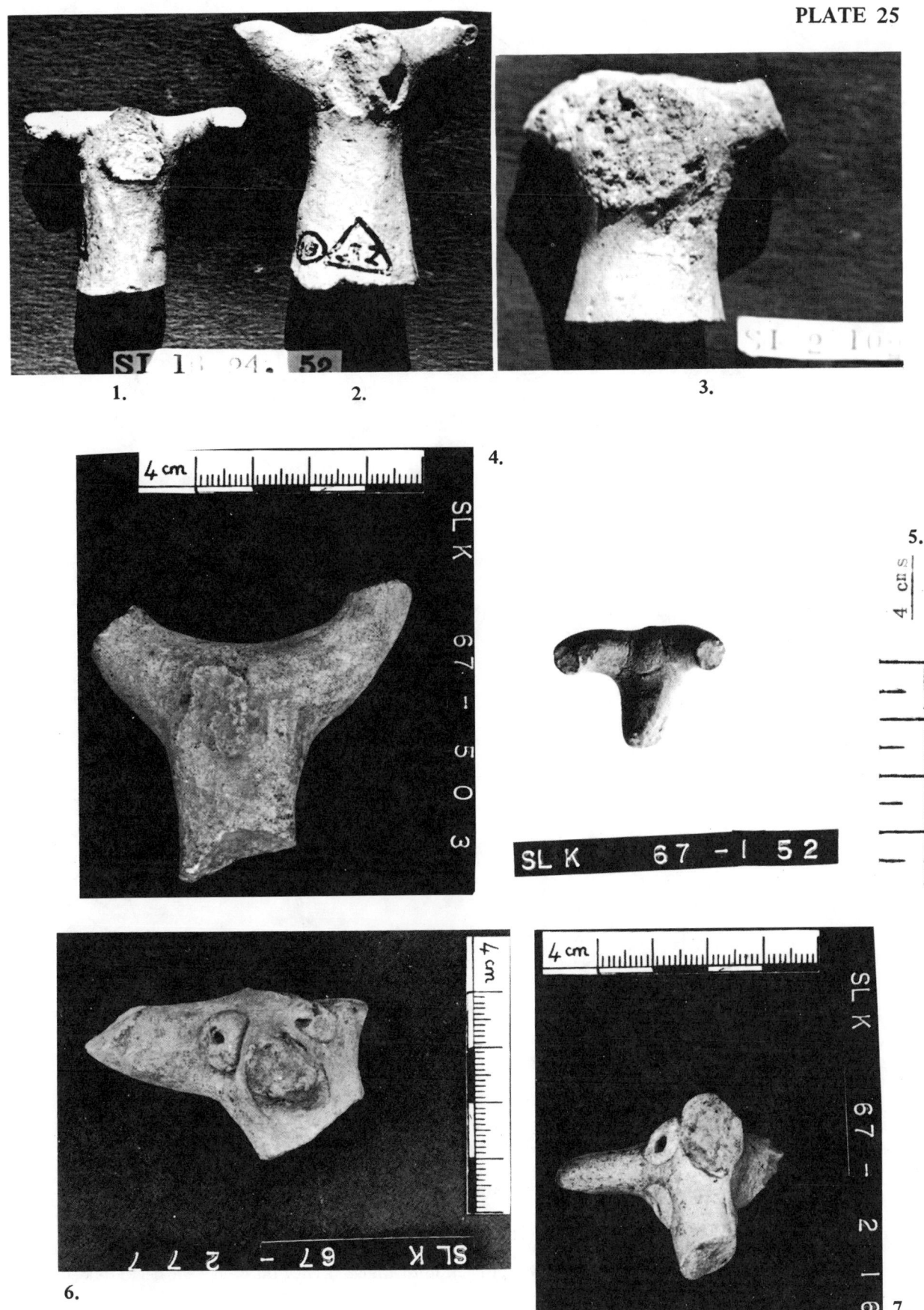

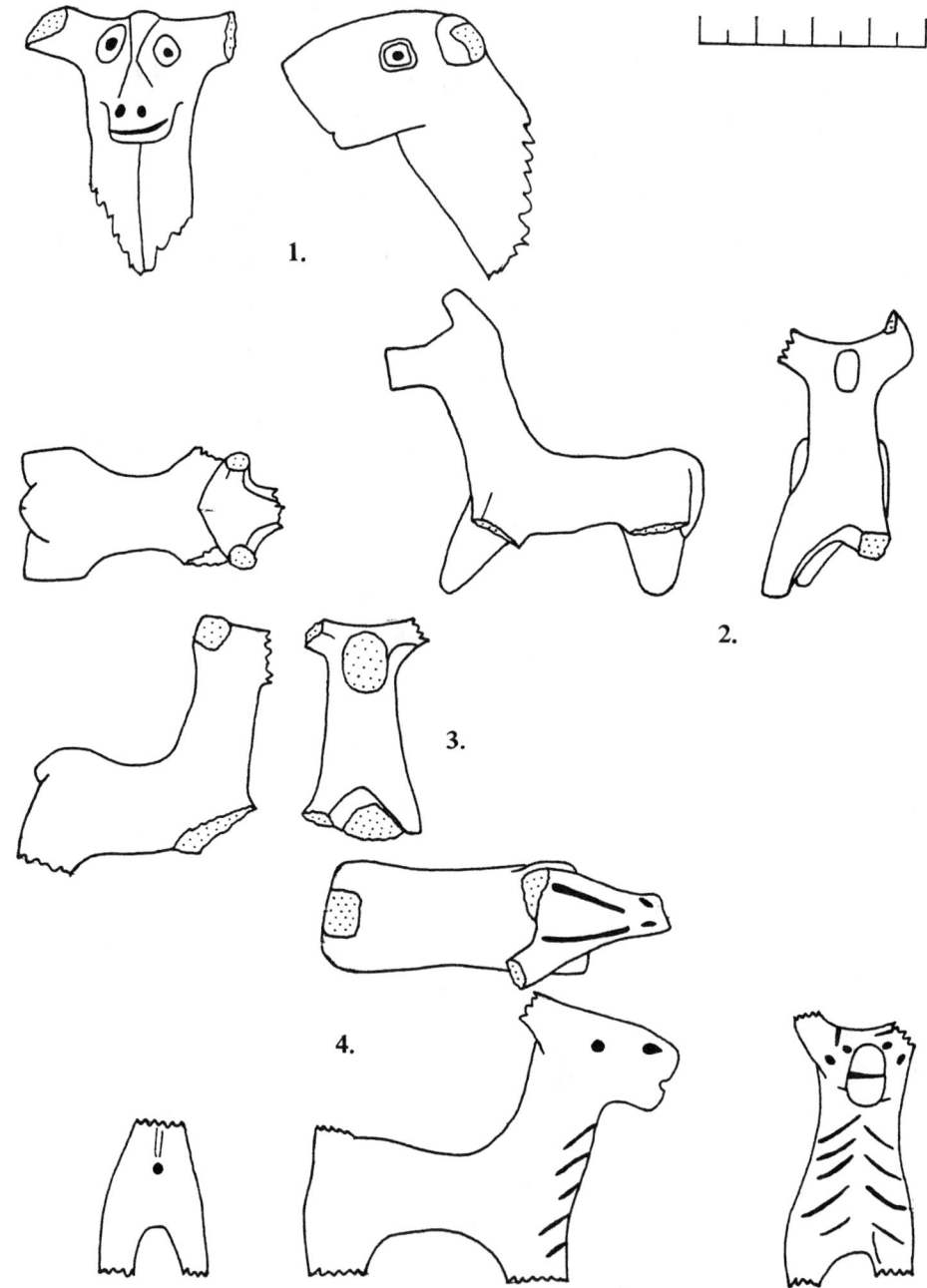

PLATE 26
Catalogue B

1. SLK 67-427, bull? Thick, blunt muzzle.

2. SLK 67-374, bull? Blunt muzzle.

3. WRD 67-44, bull? Short body.

4. SLK 67-352, goat? Swept-back horns; incised chevron design on neck; dots for nostrils and eyes.

PLATE 27

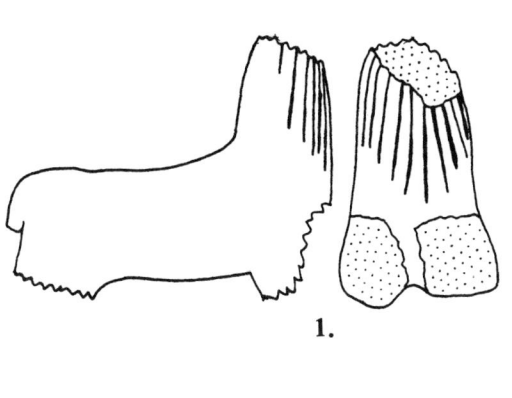

1.

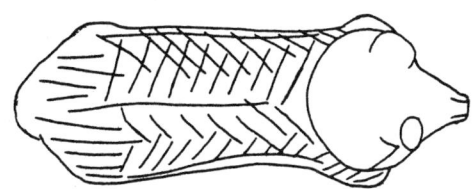

2.

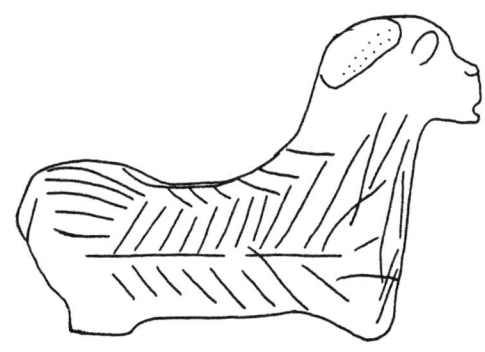

3.

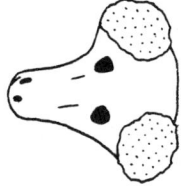

PLATE 27
Catalogue B

1. SLK 67-542, donkey? Vertical incisions on front and side of neck.

2. SLK 67-256, sheep. Incised decorations on sides and front representing animal's coat.

Uncatalogued

3. SLK 67-502, ram? Prominent horns broken away, eyes and nostrils rendered by punctures.

PLATE 28
Catalogue B

1. SLK 67-68, bird. Outspread wings, tall pedestal base.

2. SLK 67-699, bird. Highly stylized.

3. SLK 67-976, bird. Pedestal only.

Catalogue C

4. SLK 67-592, animal and rider. Erect mane on head of animal.

5. SLK 67-683, animal and rider. Body of rider contiguous with neck of animal.

6. SLK 67-685, animal and rider. Headless animal with parts of rider's legs.

7. SLK 67-955, animal and rider. Tail complete, base of erect mane.

PLATE 28

1.

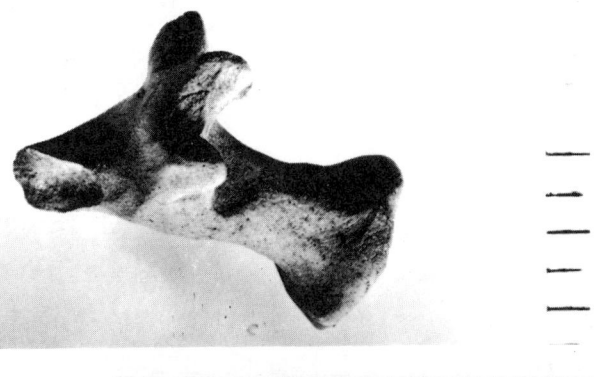

2.

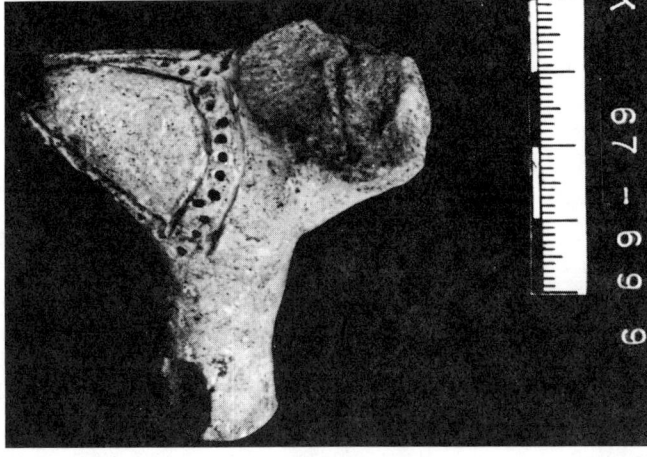

3.

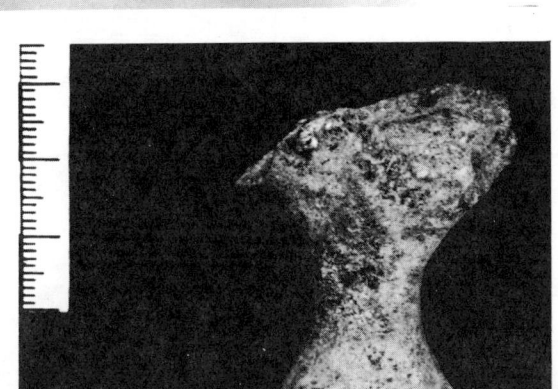

4.

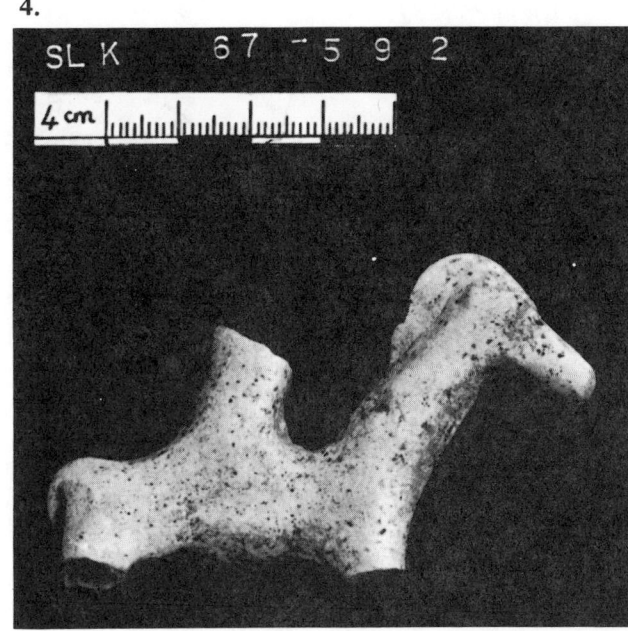

5.

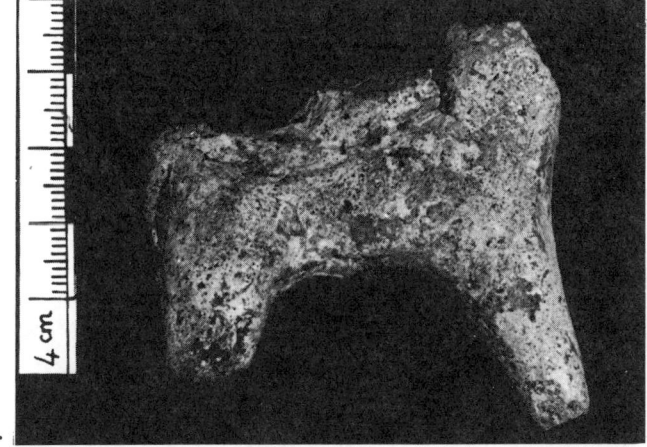

6.

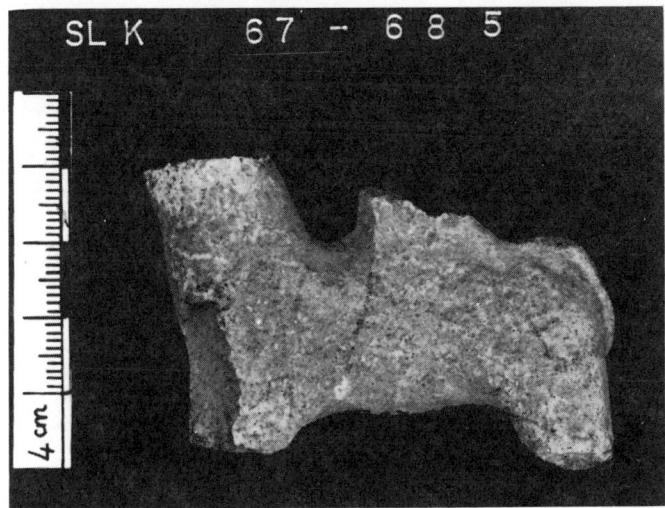

7.

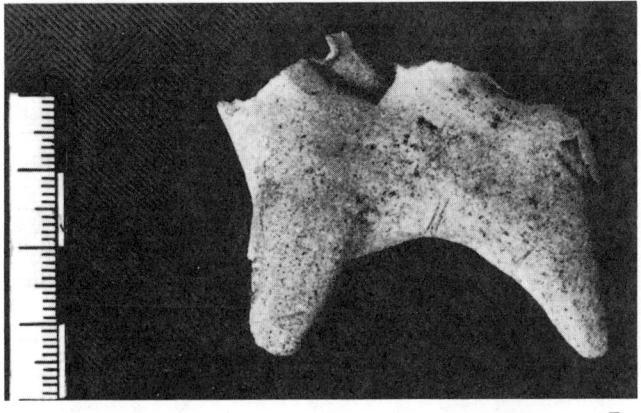

PLATE 29

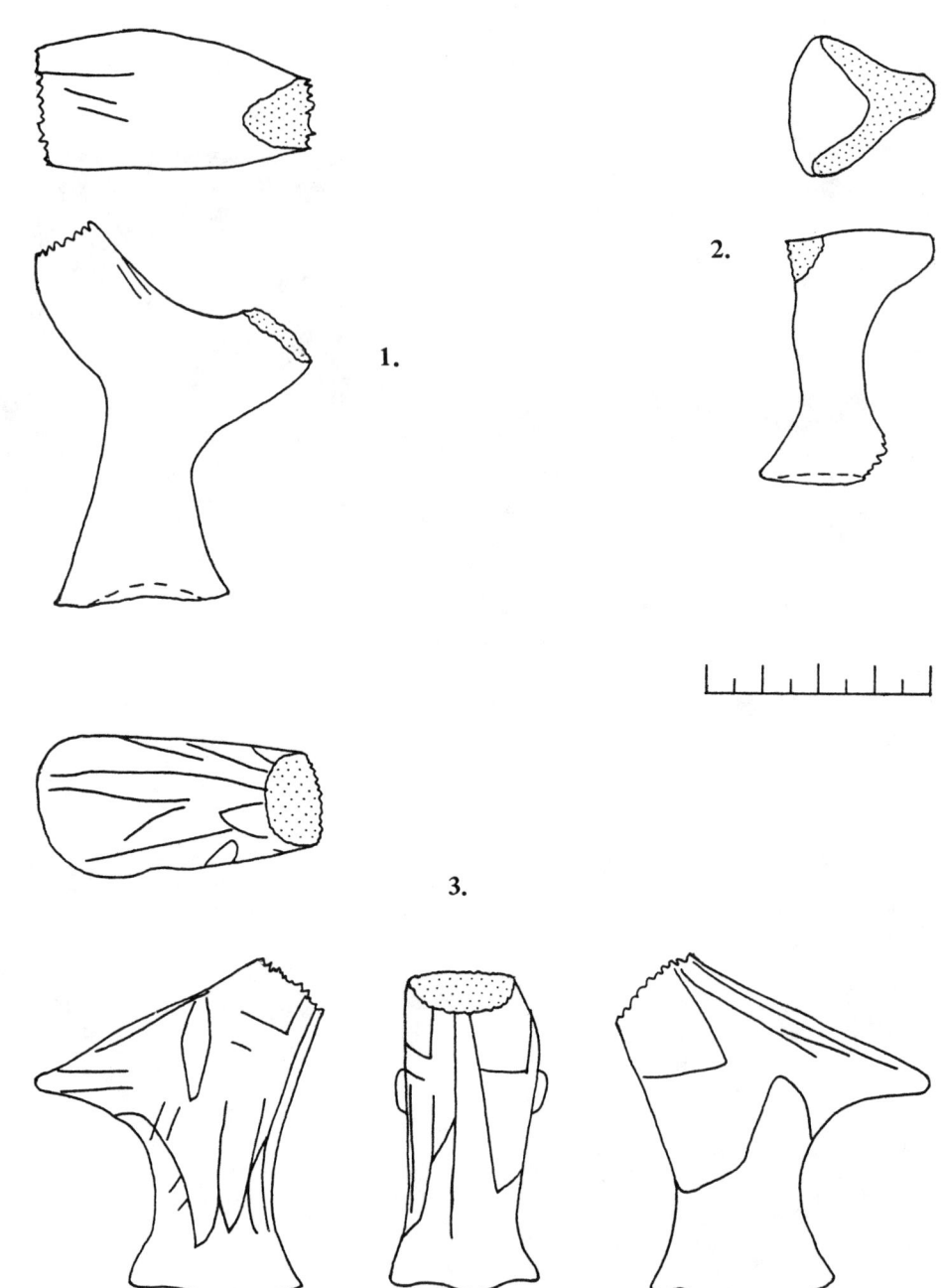

PLATE 29
Catalogue B

1. SLK 67-668, bird. Bird on pedestal base, head missing.

2. SLK 67-15, bird. Only pedestal present.

3. SLK 67-460, bird. Head missing, incised wings and plumage.

PLATE 30

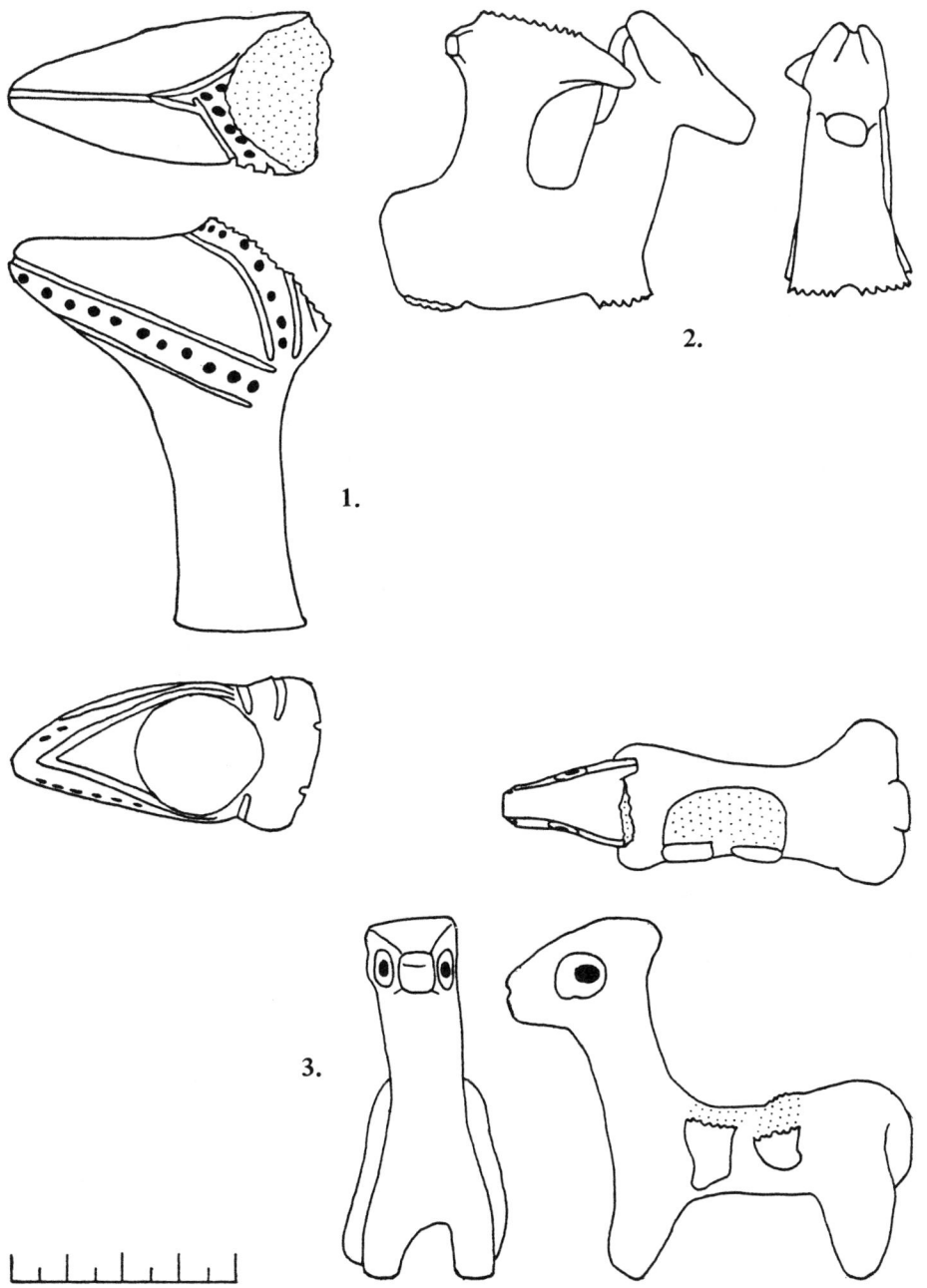

PLATE 30
Catalogue B

1. SLK 67-698, bird. Highly stylized, headless.

Catalogue C

2. SLK 67-895, animal and rider. Left arm long and extended, right short and stumpy.

3. SLK 67-206, animal and rider. Only traces of rider remain.

PLATE 30A

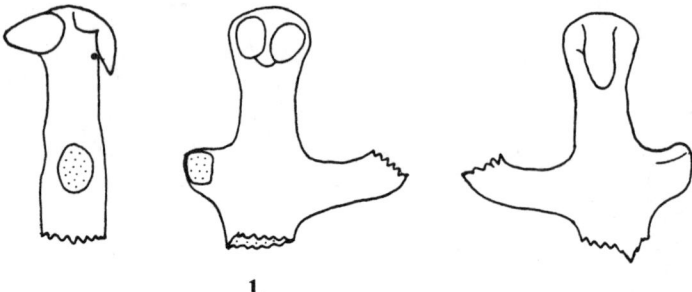

1.

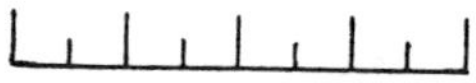

PLATE 30A
Catalogue C

1. SLK 67-1164, animal and rider. Upper part of rider figurine, extended left arm stump.

PLATE 31
Catalogue D

1. SLK 67-980, wagon. Back covered, front broken.

2. SLK 67-1248, chariot.

3. SLK 67-669, wagon.

4. SLK 67-953, chariot?

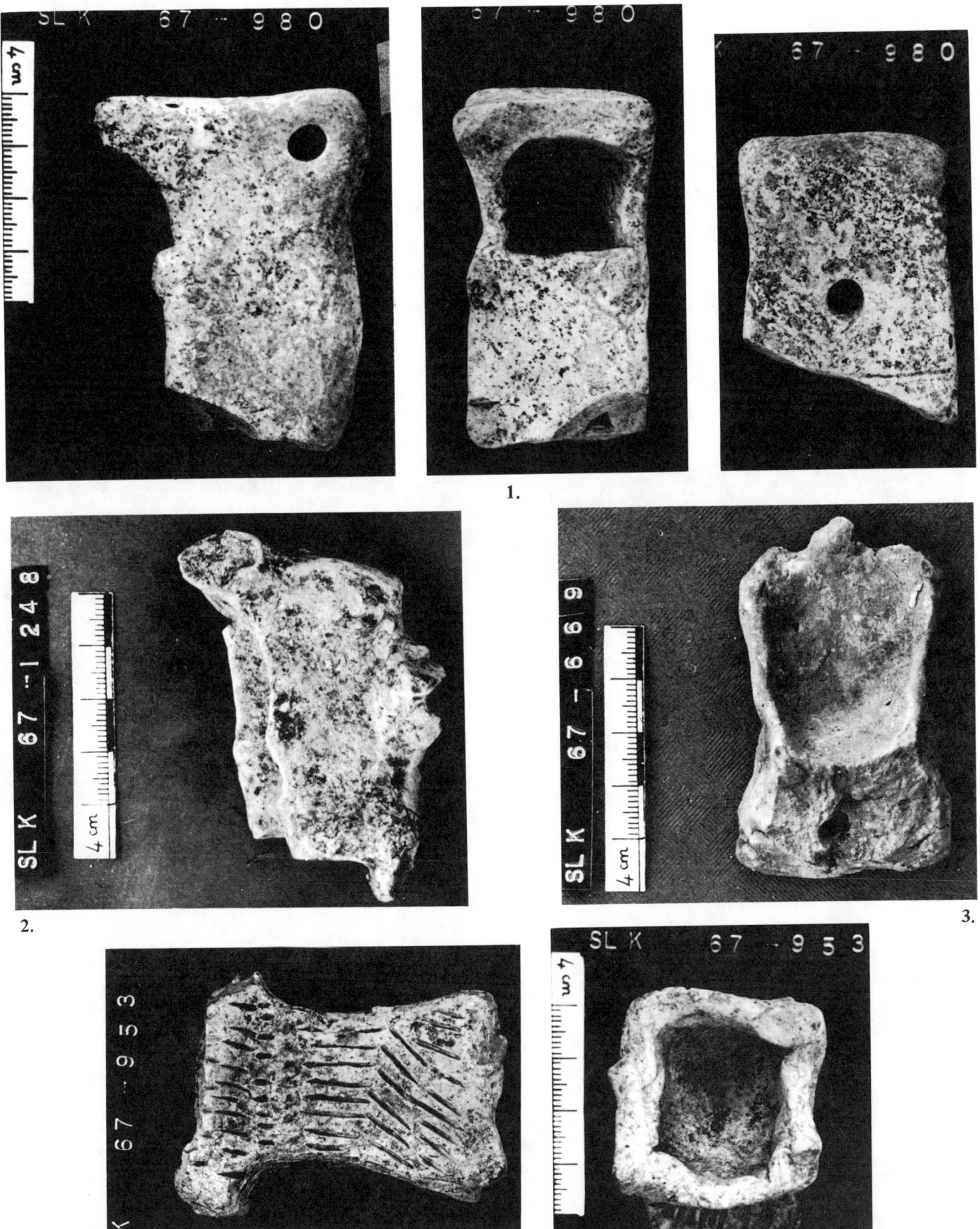

PLATE 31

PLATE 32

1.

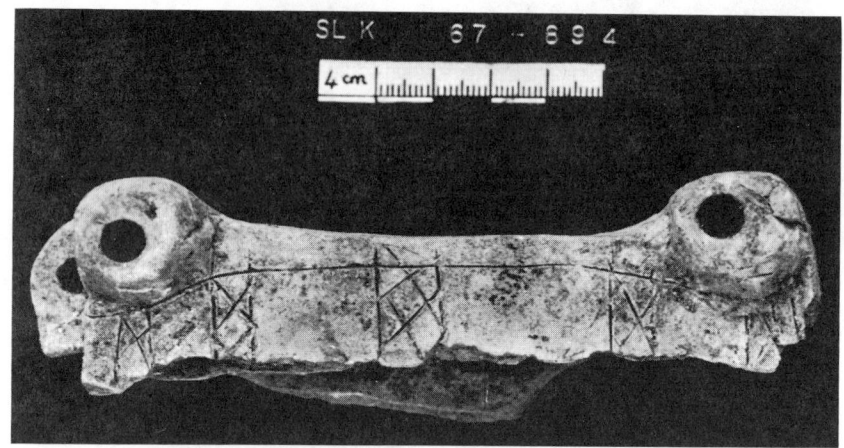

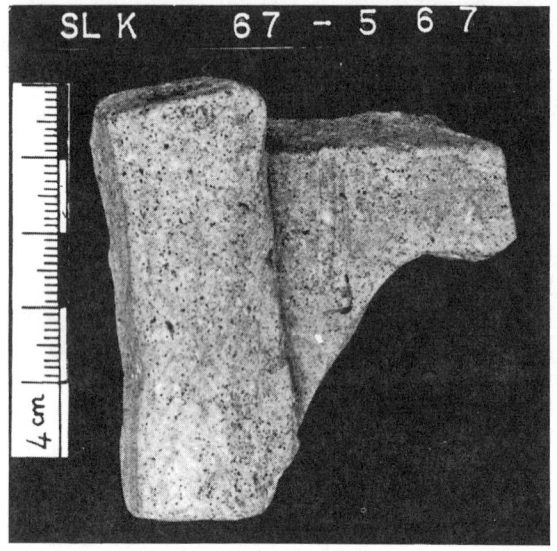

2.

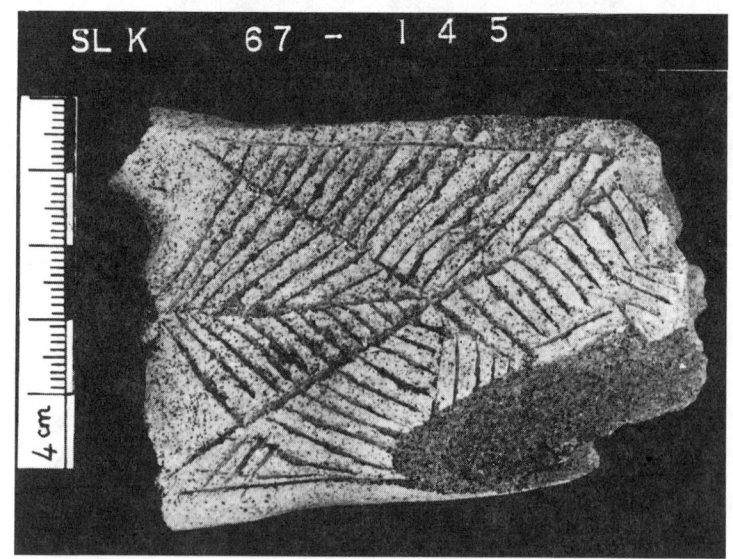

4.

3.

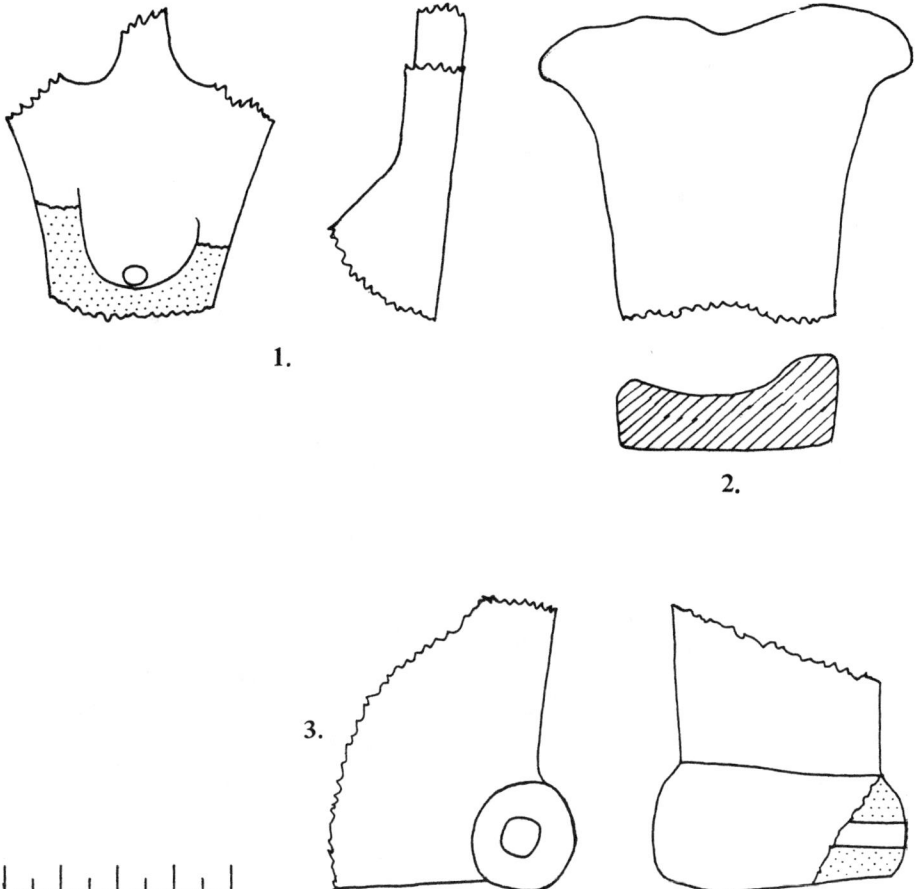

PLATE 32
Catalogue D

1. SLK 67-894, wagon. Tubular axles, ring for attachment at front end, incised decorations on sides.

2. SLK 67-567, wagon.

3. SLK 67-873, wagon. Wagon fragment.

4. SLK 67-145, chariot/wagon. Chariot/wagon fragment.

PLATE 33
Catalogue D

1. SLK 67-35, chariot/wagon. Front end with 2 apertures.

2. SLK 67-354, chariot. "Fish-tailed" front end.

3. SLK 67-33, wagon. Front bottom fragment, with axle housing.

PLATE 34

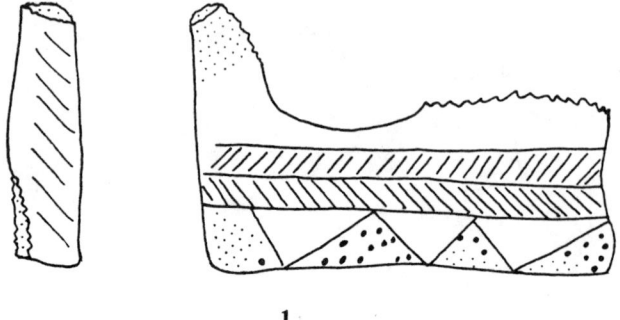

PLATE 34
Catalogue D
1. WRD 67-3, wagon. Incised with dotted triangles and herringbone pattern.